P9-AGE-533

SALINAS PUBLIC LIBRARY 11.95

649 .125 Bay   c.1

Bayard, Robert Thomas.

How to deal with your
acting-up teenager :

SALINAS PUBLIC

SALINAS
CALIFORNIA

LIBRARY

APR 2 5 1983

HOW TO DEAL WITH
YOUR ACTING-UP TEENAGER

HOW TO DEAL WITH
YOUR ACTING-UP TEENAGER

Practical Self-Help for
Desperate Parents

Robert T. Bayard, Ph.D.

Jean Bayard, Ph.D.

649.125
Bay
c.1

APR 2 5 1983

SALINAS PUBLIC
SALINAS
CALIFORNIA
LIBRARY

M. EVANS & COMPANY, INC.
New York, N.Y.

Library of Congress Cataloging in Publication Data

Bayard, Robert Thomas.
   How to deal with your acting-up teenager.

   Includes index.
   1. Parenting--United States. 2. Youth--United
States--Attitudes. 3. Conflict of generations.
I. Bayard, Jean, 1923-   . II. Title.
HQ755.85.B39 1983   649'.125   83-1414

ISBN 0-87131-407-X

Copyright © 1981, 1983 by Robert T. Bayard
     and Jean Bayard

All rights reserved. No part of this book may be
reproduced or transmitted in any form or by any
means without the written permission of the
publisher.

M. Evans and Company, Inc.
216 East 49 Street
New York, New York 10017

Manufactured in the United States of America

9 8 7 6 5 4 3 2 1

For

our beloved parents

Elsa Holwerda   Mary Bayard
Gerhardus Holwerda   Thomas Bayard

and children

Dona Sauerburger
David Bayard
Bernard Bayard
Thomas Bayard
Lynda Easley

Appreciations

Contact with some remarkable persons has helped us in developing the ideas behind this book, and in making the book itself. We are grateful:

Especially to the many desperate parents and their kids who worked as clients with us.

To Pat Kaspar, our consulting editor, and to Jane Miller, design consultant.

To Catherine Young, Ph.D., former Chief Psychologist, Western Psychiatric Institute and Clinic, University of Pittsburgh Medical School.

To Al Stratton, Ph.D., former Chief Psychologist, Staunton Clinic, University of Pittsburgh Medical School.

To Helen Mehr, Ph.D., colleague, consultant, and friend.

To Arthur Bodin, Ph.D., Research Associate, Mental Research Institute, Palo Alto.

To Richard Fisch, M.D., Paul Watzlawick, Ph.D. and John Weakland, of the Brief Therapy Group, Mental Research Institute, Palo Alto.

And to our colleagues of the Emergency Treatment Center, Santa Clara:

Diana Everstine, Ph.D., Director

Ellen Bader, Ph.D.

Mike Barraza, M.S.

Ione Binford, M.S.

Carolyn Cameron, M.S.

Fred D'Aguinaga

Christine Dusek, M.S.

Louis Everstine, Ph.D.

Stephen Fields, Ph.D.

Edith Groner, M.S.W.

Harold Johnson, Ph.D.

Margaret Johnson

Novelle Johnson, M.S.

Ferol Larsen, M.A.

Jay Livingston, Ph.D.

Marcia Porter, Ph.D.

David Rasch, M.S.

Christine Remus, M.A.

Sheri Rosso

Edith Savage

David Fenstermaker, M.S.

Manoucher Tavokoli, Ph.D.

Richard Toft, Ph.D.

Judy Tombrink, M.S.

Matthew Turnbo, M.S.

Eileen Valcov, Ph.D.

Deak Van Arsdale, Ph.D.

Madelyn Witt, M.S.

Contents

Preface   xi

Chapter 1.   GETTING THE PROBLEM INTO
             PERSPECTIVE   1

Common teenage problems and traditional
responses. . .What you can accomplish with
the help of this book. . .Six reassuring truths
behind the parent/teen dilemma. . .Defining
short and long term goals for change

Chapter 2.   GIVING YOUR KID RESPONSIBILITY
             FOR HIS/HER OWN LIFE.   15

Two sets of problems: those that affect your
kid's life versus those that upset yours. . .
How to go about giving your kid this
responsibility

Chapter 3.   WHY IT IS SO HARD TO GIVE YOUR
             KID RESPONSIBILITY   37

The "good parent" fallacy. . .The trouble
with shoulds and should-nots. . .Letting
your teenager make his/her own decisions
. . .What you believe about your kid will
come true

Chapter 4. HOW YOUR KID MAY RESPOND   52

The teenager's wish for and fear of
freedom. . .Handling conflict. . .How not
to give in to the demand for negative
attention

Chapter 5. TAKING BACK RESPONSIBILITY
           FOR YOUR OWN LIFE   67

Getting back in touch with your own wants
and needs. . .Seven exercises to sharpen
your response to your inner voice

Chapter 6. PREPARING TO STAND UP.   85

Getting past the doormat attitude. . .
Your rights and how to claim them. . .
How to overcome fear of encounter

Chapter 7. ELIMINATING TRIGGERS AND
           REINFORCERS   102

A change of tactics for tough problems:
lying, stealing, threats, swearing, a sullen
or belligerent attitude, when your kid
abuses favors

Chapter 8. STANDING UP FOR YOURSELF   126

A five-step campaign. . .Establishing a
fair request for change. . .Standing firm
against pressure. . .Sample dialogues for
specific problems

Chapter 9. FOLLOWING THROUGH ON YOUR
           STAND   147

How to steal center stage from your
teenager. . .Becoming spontaneous. . .
Establishing credibility. . .The Parental
Strike

Chapter 10. A LOOK AHEAD 175

    You and your kid in the future

Appendix A. QUESTIONS PARENTS ASK 180

Appendix B. SOME PARENTS AND HOW
                THEY COPED 185

Index 203

Preface

If you are feeling worried or troubled about your teenager, we want to extend to you a welcome and to share with you, through this book, a way of easing your load. Do not feel alone, for there are thousands of other parents experiencing much the same problems you are, and the chances are that some of them are very close to you— near neighbors and friends. You may not realize you have this much company, because in our society the parent is "supposed to" feel ashamed when a son or daughter cuts school or gets drunk or otherwise behaves foolishly, and therefore even friends tend not to confide in each other how their kids are really doing and how they, the parents, really feel about it. Your friends, to show a polite interest in you, may still greet you with the question "How are the kids?" but the appropriate answer is to tell them about the socially-approved things your kids are doing, not about the rebellions, the fights, the late nights, the truancies. To let the negative things become known would somehow mark you a failure as a parent, and the others you know feel the same way about it, so everyone keeps quiet and feels desperate in private.

We, Bob and Jean Bayard, have gone through this

kind of experience, and so feel a special kind of interest in the situation of beleaguered parents. To us, it's vitally important which of two ways you go in resolving that situation. It will almost certainly look as if the problem originates in something your kid is doing, and as if the solution lies in somehow changing your kid, getting him or her to behave differently; however it will almost as certainly be better handled by seeing it as an opportunity for you to change something about your life, expanding it and learning to take better care of it. In this book we give you our ideas on how to take the second way, for the benefit of you *and* your kid.

We did not always feel so confident about how to handle these situations as we do now. We have raised five children, and in the process we have done almost every one of the things, either wise or foolish, that we talk about in this book. The kinds of things our children did is their story to tell, and we respect their privacy, so we will say only that we have probably lived through as wide a gamut of kid behavior as any of the parents we have worked with, and our feelings about it colored our lives for many years.

After raising our first two children nearly to adulthood, we seemed still to have plenty of fatherly-motherly feeling left. (Did we also want to prove we could be good parents and therefore worthwhile persons?) At any rate, it was with joy and a sense of adventure that we adopted three more children, an eleven year old and two five year olds, from Korea. By the time all five were grown and ready to go on their own, we had had thirty consecutive years of kid raising.

Our experience during that period was one of ups and downs. There were times when the kids were "doing fine" and then we felt fine, too. At other times they did the kinds of things we talk about in this book, and then we felt unhappy—hurt, angry, and trapped. Every incident of this sort that came up touched off some basic, very uncomfortable feelings in the two of us. For Bob it was ideas like:

There is something wrong with me.

I can't establish a good, close relationship with my kids.

They do not see me as a person.

For Jean it was a feeling of guilt and dread:

I must be a bad person.

I should be giving my whole life to the children. Instead, I am going to school or working part time. This is depriving them in some terrible way, and that's why they're misbehaving.

We were both ashamed of these feelings and suffered alone with them for a long time. Much later we came to see them as simply poor habits of thinking which we believe many parents in our society become caught in, and which can very well be changed.

To help with all the difficulty we were experiencing in kid-raising we tried everything we could find that held out any hope for us.

We read books on child-raising. Some were very good; however most of them touched off our guilt because they talked only about what parents could do for the child's sake, and we read into this the implication that our own lives should not matter.

We took kids to expensive psychotherapy sessions for years. Probably this helped in some way, but the main result we *saw* was that our kids came to believe they were "patients", had something wrong with them, and needed help to get going on anything in life. We were so ashamed of having to resort to counseling that we never told any of our relatives or friends.

We took a class based on Dr. Thomas Gordon's Parent Effectiveness Training book. This was the first real help we experienced. It gave us a start at becoming equal members in our own family, and at seeing our kids as interesting and worthwhile responsible persons.

We studied family life and psychotherapy at the university, and took advanced degrees in psychology.

We began working as professional counselors for teenagers and their families who were in crisis. By now we have worked with hundreds and hundreds of vulnerable, rebellious, angry, sad, or determined teenagers and their (usually) desperate parents. Much of what we see in these situations seems familiar to us, and we feel that we understand it.

We have noticed in doing this crisis work that it is usually the parents who are worried when things seem to go wrong. Very occasionally a few kids call us for help in getting off drugs or alcohol, for instance, but very, very few ask for help because they are associating with the wrong friends, lying, stealing, cutting school, running away, etc. When kids do these things, it is the parents who become desperate and call for help. That's why we're addressing this book to them.

We thought, worked, agonized, coped, over raising our five. We had crescendos of weeping and high hopes, of despair and jubilation, of helplessness and triumph. All of these intensified as each kid became a teenager and hit, as we experienced it. a peak of being impossible to live with. We struggled earnestly through it all.

Eventually—and here is a note of beautiful hope we'd like to sound for every parent—the struggle began to ease. We began to notice, every once in a while, that we were actually at ease with our children, and about our children. Humor began to creep in; some of the things they said and did began to strike us as so human and so imbued with pathos that we understood them and had to smile even as we shook our heads and worried. Positive things that pleasantly surprised us began to happen more and more often; our kids let us know, in meaningful ways, that they loved us, and every one of them did good and noble things of the sort that parents feel proud about. We found ourselves feeling utterly content with our kids.

For a while we thought that this came about because they were finally maturing. Of course, they were but it's only lately that we have realized that we have changed. Our children were always loyal and sneaky, kind and inconsiderate, caring and selfish. As they matured they of course changed in many ways, but as far as our relationship to them goes, we started out wanting something of them—that they turn out a certain way—and they have served as our patient teachers, doing the exact things that were needed to wean us from those expectations and free us to be able to enjoy them as they are. We feel a considerable debt to the experience we've had together. Without it, we might have gone all our lives with the same cozy but rigid expectations. They helped us enter a larger world.

That is the main contribution we feel we can make in this book—to encourage you, the parent, to see the present trouble with your kid not so much as evidence of a bad or mistaken kid, but as a pressure upon you to expand and to change, and a chance to do so. Despite the pain, it's possible for you even to welcome this problem as one of the challenges, not of your kid's, but of *your* life.

We can't of course pretend to have "the answers" for a given situation, but we've had a lot of experience, we care about the happiness and responsibility of parents and kids, and we can tell you what we'd be likely to try in your situation. We believe that the approach we describe, if you follow it, can make a large and happy change in your situation.

At times it will probably be difficult, even scary.

It will require some changes in the way you think.

It may be exhilarating, too, and give you a sense of expansion and liberation.

We suggest that you spend a couple of evenings reading through the book—the text, exercises, examples, and all—in a very relaxed way, just reading it through to let yourself get a general flavor of hopefulness, ease, and a sense that things will be all right. Then start again at the beginning and work through each step in turn. We suggest working through the book in order because it would not be good to do the things at the end of the book without building up a background based on the earlier portion.

And—be kind to yourself. We can understand if you can't do some of the things we suggest, because we too were unable to do some of it in crises with our children. If we had it to do over again, knowing what we know now, we'd definitely follow our own advice, but we had to come through some hard learning and we made many mistakes. We forgive ourselves and hope you'll forgive yourself for whatever you can't do. Our hope is that you simply feel good about whatever things you can do, and that by reading this book you become a little more yourself and a little more able to change.

One

Getting the Problem

into Perspective

This is a difficult time for you. You're upset, worried, maybe angry about something your teenager is doing.
It may be something private and very small in the eyes of the world.

Jody doesn't seem to have any self-confidence. She spends most of her time in her room and at dinnertime she hardly talks with us.

It may be big enough that others in the community —school, police—are involved in it.

Dan's been picked up by the police for driving someone's car without a license.

In any case it looms large for you and it has you worried about how your kid is turning out, what he or she will do next, and perhaps how you yourself will be able to stand living with this person until he or she reaches adulthood.
It may be any of the following things, all of which we've heard worried, caring parents complain about:

1

Tom (14) steals money, liquor, jewelry from us.

Jan (13) stays out until all hours or even all night if she feels like it.

He (17) won't do anything around the house. He leaves messes in his room, in the kitchen, all over, and will not clean them up.

I know Linda (14) is on pot.

She (12) goes with raunchy older friends who have nothing going for them and just hang around like shiftless bums.

Ann (16) has had two abortions. Now she's pregnant for the third time.

Jerry (14) joined Boy Scouts and as soon as I paid for the uniform, he dropped out.

It's the lying I can't stand. I can't trust anything Karen (14) tells me to be the truth.

Maurice (15) won't go to school; he hasn't gone more than a few weeks in the last two years.

Meredith (12) has been arrested for shoplifting.

Donna (17) always wants to be by herself. She spends hours alone in her room.

He (16) won't be part of the family. He won't go anywhere with us and mostly he won't even talk with us.

My son (14) ran away; he's been at his friend's house for six days.

It's the four-letter words. Dave (13) calls me names no boy ought even to say in front of his mother.

These things are naturally frightening to most parents, who take them to mean:

My son or daughter will turn out badly

and

I have been a bad parent

as well as, perhaps:

My kid doesn't love me.

People will know I failed.

He or she has won over me.

I'm trapped to live like this with this person for another three (or five, or seven) years, and there's no way out.

Besides having these kinds of painful thoughts, you may be feeling extremely discouraged because it seems there is nothing you can do about the situation. You may have tried everything you could think of only to find that none of it helped for very long. You've tried to discipline him or her.

All right, you're grounded.

You did it again, so now you're grounded for the whole summer!

Or "rewards."

I'll give you five dollars if you don't miss any school this week.

I'll fix you an afternoon treat if you'll change your school clothes.

Or common sense parental guidance and orders.

Anne, you should go to school and do your homework. If you don't, you won't be able to get a decent job later and you'll wish you had.

It's not right to steal, and you should not do it.

Don't treat your mother that way.

You may have tried direct supervision.

I'm going to get you up at 6:30, drive you to school, escort you to your class, and pick you up right after school.

You may have decided that perhaps your kid needed understanding and love, and tried heart-to-heart talks and reassuring him or her that you care.

Carl, why do you do these things? Let's talk about it.

I love you.

You may have taken your kid for "counseling," only to find that things improved for a time and then deteriorated again, or even that things didn't improve at all, or that your kid refused to go.

You may well have the feeling that you've tried every approach society has offered you and since none of them worked, there must be something lacking in you.

What am I doing wrong? Where have I failed?

I should have been here when you were little.

Maybe it's because you have only one parent; I deprived you of your father (or mother) by getting divorced.

And so on.

All of this makes for an extremely painful situation for a parent. It *hurts* to feel worried, helpless, humiliated, guilty. It is this pain we are addressing in this book. We want to tell you it may not be necessary for you to hurt in this way.

We believe that if you sincerely work on the approach we've outlined for you in this book, you can bring yourself into a happier situation, and at the same time do the most that is possible for you to do toward your teenager's best development.

As a matter of fact, there may even be positive aspects to your painful situation right now. The worse the problem you're having with your teenager, the more likely you are to be hurting badly, and therefore the more energy you may be willing to put into working on the problem and into changing. We will be asking you to try some different ways of doing things, even of thinking, and it's often tempting to slough off such suggestions. Your hurting and desperation may motivate you to try some of these new things and thereby be the cause of your breaking into an expanded and happier way of being for you and for your kid.

Let's assume then that you're disturbed about something your teenager is doing, and want a way of proceeding. We're going to describe such a way in five or six steps, with a chapter or two to cover each step. We suggest that you take each step seriously and spend some time on it before going on to the next one, for each step is based upon your having some mastery of all preceding steps. You might just browse quickly through the whole book first to get an idea of the total, but then we recommend settling down and working through each step in order. As we see it, you're in a painful situation which has taken a long time and a great deal of input from all family members to build up, and it won't be resolved by throwing in a few superficial techniques. On the other hand, given an honest commitment on your part to work on it seriously and *persistently*, step by step, it seems reasonable that you should see some difference in the way things go within six to eight weeks. A sustained effort of several months would probably result in still further improvement.

Before we begin—a note on levels of parental participation. If you are a single parent, your effort alone will almost certainly yield positive results. If there are two parents involved in the upbringing of the kid or kids in question, it is a definite plus when both take the approach presented in this book. However if your partner declines to participate, it is still quite feasible for you to do it alone. In any case our experience shows that as long as any parent makes a sincere and sustained effort along the lines we are suggesting in this book, improvements will be achieved.

We are now ready to begin. The first step is to hearten yourself. We find that it is important, in working to improve the situation with your kid, that you allow yourself to become encouraged about this possibility by learning to relax, getting a perspective on your situation, and generally acquiring a degree of inner peacefulness. When you're feeling worried, upset, angry, you are likely to act impulsively and do things that actually get you the reverse of what you truly want. So now we ask you to spend a few minutes getting yourself into a most proper mood for achieving something positive. You'll do best if you operate from a place of inner peace and relaxation.

You may have your own ways of doing this; perhaps you meditate regularly, for example, or find that walking a few miles or giving yourself a half hour to be alone without demands relaxes you and gives you a wider perspective. You may do some regular exercise that leaves you feeling fresh and relaxed. If so, we ask you to do this for yourself before you begin working through this book and to repeat it every time you find yourself in difficulties. In case you'd like to try some of our ways of self-heartening, we're including here some exercises we find to be helpful. They may strike you as simple; don't let that blind you to the fact that if you give yourself to them, they can be very powerful. We find that only one factor really prevents a person from successfully heartening him or herself, and that is *failure to understand that*

it can be done. Most people do not realize that they themselves make their own moods, and that therefore they can
change them, and that it is all right for them to change
them. If you give yourself permission, you can put yourself into a calm, everything-is-basically-all-right-and-now-
let's-see-what-I-can-do-about-this-problem, mood. We've
seen people do it, and we've done it ourselves, and therefore we believe you have the ability to do it.

In order to hearten yourself then before going on to
direct work with the kid problem, go through the following
sequence of exercises.

Exercise One

Right now, while sitting in your chair, learn how to
relax your muscles, all of them except the few needed to
stay sitting and hold your book.

One of the strange habits most adults develop is that
of tightening muscles when we get into uncomfortable or
stressful situations. It's a strange habit because the tight-
ened muscles do not forward our getting out of the bad
situation; instead they tend to lock us even more tightly
into it. It's well worth learning exactly the reverse response: *relaxing* our muscles whenever discomfort or stress
arises. Doing this puts us into a far better position to
resolve and change the problem.

With practice you will be able to relax quite thoroughly in a second or two. However, if you think of it as
something that only takes that much time we can almost
guarantee you will see it as unimportant, maybe try it a
time or two, and then drop it entirely. Therefore we ask
you to do a more systematic relaxing now and to do it
again and again in the coming days and weeks until it is
second nature for you, every time you become aware of
any problem arising, to let go all muscles that are unnecessarily tense. Relaxing your muscles will make it almost
impossible for the situation with your kid to go on as it
has been, if only because you will not be able to respond
in that situation as you have been doing. It's possible you

can't even get angry or worry if you're thoroughly relaxed.
Relaxing your muscles can also be extremely valuable for
your physical health.

Right now, then, as you're sitting in your chair, first
tense up every muscle in your body at once, as tightly
as you can, and hold the tenseness ten seconds or so.
Sit there as tensed and rigid as you can get. Then let it
all go—let your body sag limp into your chair. Notice how
this feels, how the next breath after you let go tends to
be slow and deep, and how you can then feel the tension
leaving, draining away.

Now, continuing to sit quietly in your chair, spend
at least ten minutes deepening the relaxation by mentally
going over every part of your body and letting it relax even
farther. As you do, let a feeling of inner peacefulness
spread throughout your body as you give each part permission to relax.

"Now toes are relaxing (as you let them go even more
limp). Now, the arches of my feet are relaxing. Now, the
heels. Now, the ankles are letting go and relaxing. Now
my calf and shin muscles are relaxing still more."

Continue thus, slowly and gently, over your entire
body, returning to specific areas as needed until you can
feel a satisfying degree of relaxation throughout your body.

Now, gently continuing with any sense of relaxation
you achieved, and using only the muscles you need to hold
your book and read, go on to the next exercise.

Exercise Two

Sitting quietly, imagine now that there is a little piece
of you, at the very center of your being, which is very,
very calm and happy. Undisturbed by all the worries and
the fears about the future, there it sits, utterly peaceful,
strong, and happy. It cannot be touched. Picture it in terms
of some image if you wish—a flame, a jewel, or a secret
lake, calm, smooth, and without a ripple. Imbue it with a
profound peacefulness and joy, a stillness; realize it is
safe and strong. There it is, deep inside you. Imagine you

are this flame or this jewel or this lake, deep at the core of yourself.

Imagine that this secret center is going to be there within you always, staying there, calm and still, through all the tasks and problems and worries you will go through and that if you wish, *you can learn to remember it is there.* It is a little core of inner peace, and many times, as you go through your day, you can remember it and mentally touch it. Knowing it is there you can feel strengthened and relaxed for the encounters with your kid which are to come.

Exercise Three

Now, holding the feeling of relaxation and of an inner peace, begin gently to expand your view of the world so that the problem with your kid shrinks to a manageable size within that view. If you've been feeling worry or resentment or other painful emotions when you think of this problem you have probably come to see it within a limited framework—a framework which is simultaneously limiting your creativity in working out solutions to the problem. You'll have more space with a widened perspective.

While remaining very relaxed, then, sit comfortably in your chair and let your thoughts dwell on the problem with your son or daughter. Picture you and him or her in this worrisome situation. When you have this well in mind, think of both of you and the home you live in, along with anyone else who lives with you, so that you're now thinking of yourself and your kid and whomever else may live there, all in your home.

Now, add the immediate neighborhood. Think of the land and the little group of buildings that make up your neighborhood, and all the people there—you and your teenager and your neighborhood and all the people in it. When this picture is clear in your mind, back up still farther and think of the whole state—you, your kid, and all these other hundreds of parents and kids and other people working and interacting, and all this stretch of land. Enlarging it further, think of your whole country, millions of people and families, millions of acres of land, cities, fields. Having thought this far, now picture for yourself the whole earth, the land and the oceans and the people. Backing now much farther away, let yourself think of the whole earth and all the rest of the solar system—a vast burning sun and massive planets, moons, cosmic dust wheeling slowly around it. Imagine now the entire galaxy—whole clusters of solar systems, stretching out so far you can get a grasp on the distances between them only by marvelling at them. Then let yourself imagine the universe—millions of galaxies spread out in all directions, to an end no human being has yet imagined.

Now, continuing to hold in mind the sense of this immensity of being, come back to think of the problem with your son or daughter, and assign it its proper importance in the scheme of things. Realize that yes, it is a real, tangible problem—and yes, in all this vastness of being, you can probably trust it to work itself out somehow, no matter what you do, without resulting in any real or lasting damage in our total world.

Exercise Four

Imagine that you are on a very relaxed vacation in Italy, and that you are browsing through the ruins of the ancient city of Pompeii. It is a calm, sunny day. As you look around, you see on all sides the evidences of the everyday life of the past—streets and rows of fallen houses, patios, kitchens, stone wine casks. Hundreds of years ago people worked, talked, raised families, in this place which is now very still, basking in the warm sun. Imagine that in this quiet place you now come upon a stone column on which some householder of the ancient city recorded the events of his daily life, and you see written there: "Today I was filled with dread and anger because my son was picked up by the Pompeii police"—or, "Today I realized that my daughter is using hashish."

Notice how much or how little adrenalin you generate

at the thought of that parent's dilemma in that long ago time. It may be that you experience a certain compassion and fellow feeling for him or her, but very little real anxiety.

Now imagine that you were that householder, that it is your problem with your kid that is inscribed on the stone column, and that nearly 2000 years have passed since it all happened. Notice how you feel about the problem in this light.

Now, in your present, nicely relaxed frame of mind, continue reading and consider with us some important facts:

Most kids who do the kinds of things we listed at the beginning of this chapter turn out OK; that is to say, as adults, they manage to support themselves and carry their own weight in the world while maintaining reasonably comfortable relationships with others in their lives, including their parents. The probability is that no matter how worried, angry, despairing you have been feeling about it, the situation will improve and your kid will turn out to be a reasonably decent and happy person.

Most families go through a period during a son's or daughter's adolescence in which parents and kids have trouble living together. Most kids, including the ones who do the things we've listed above, make a psychological return later—usually sometime between eighteen and twenty-five—*and become friends with their parents.*

You have lots of company. Thousands of parents are going through what you are, right now, and more thousands have gone through it in the past and come out on the other side.

You probably have not ruined your kid even if you're thinking with a great deal of guilt that you have been a "bad parent." There is a tremendous force in kids—as in people in general—which presses to fulfill their lives, and this force, more than anything you could do or not do, determines how they turn out. It is clear that there is a great range of different environments in which kids can grow up successfully—in Central American villages in which they're isolated in dark huts for their earliest years, in Eskimo igloos, in native tribes in which they're raised by other children or the village adults in general and rarely see their parents.

If you're feeling trapped, resentful, and that your kid has won over you, you almost certainly have more power than you think you have, including the power to change things around so that you feel better. Doing this, far from being destructive to the kid, would probably be beneficial for both him or her, and you.

Here is a final daring thought you might consider:

You have as much need for and right to happiness, freedom, consideration, love, and so on, as your kid does.

We'll assume you're feeling ready now to begin working on the specific problem you're having with your kid. First, let's look to see exactly what your goal is. What is it you're after in relation to your son or daughter? If you can clarify and hold in mind what you want as you interact with him or her, you can be more sure you're heading toward it and not simply digging yourself more deeply into the present stressed situation, which you don't want. What exactly is your goal in this situation?

Parents in this kind of situation are usually after several things at once, at different levels. At the most immediate, specific level, they're after getting the kid to change the particular behavior that is worrisome.

He can't go on stealing!

He's got to go to school!

I want her to come in on time!

I want her to stop using four letter words!

When asked to consider why they want these particular changes, parents are likely to respond with further goals at a somewhat more general level. For example,

I want him to quit stealing because:

I want him to be an honest person.

I want him not to get into trouble.

He should go to school because:

I want him to graduate from high school.

I want him to be able to get a good job.

She should come in on time because:

I want her not to get in trouble out there.

Then, when they are asked what they are after in the most long term way, why they're going through the many years of kid raising, they describe very general goals.

I want him to turn out to be a good person.

I want her to be happy.

I want him to have good relationships with other people in his life.

If we summarize and bring to the highest level what most parents seem to be after, the following goal covers most of it:

I want my kid to turn out to be a decent, responsible person, able to make good decisions for him or herself.

Now, we have noticed something interesting about the process of achieving goals in interpersonal situations like the one between you and your teenager. We find that it works best and gives you the greatest chance of attaining your goals at all levels if you forget about the lower level goals for the time being and direct your energies toward achieving the highest goal. In fact, you cannot attain many of the lower level goals by going after them directly, and attempts to do so tend to worsen rather than improve them. Trying to make your kid stop stealing, or go to school, may only lead to increased stealing or truancy especially when, as is often the case, the kid gets attention by doing them. However, these same lower level goals frequently fall into place when you aim toward the higher goal. For this reason we ask you to set aside the more immediate concerns for the moment—your worry over the current crisis, the specific situation with the school or the stealing or the undesirable friends. Instead, take the long view in your dealings with your son or daughter. In deciding how to behave in interactions with your kid, drop that urge to push him or her to shape up in the specific situation and instead, ask yourself, "What can I do in this situation that would contribute to my kid's being more responsible and able to make his or her own decisions?"

Two

Giving Your Kid Responsibility

for His or Her Own Life

At this point we are going to introduce some ideas which, if you are having trouble with your kid, may surprise you—may strike you as selfish, or immoral, or revolutionary. If this is your reaction, we ask you to withhold judgment on these ideas until you have read through the whole book and understand our viewpoint, because, even though they may take some getting used to, we find them to be both humane and effective.

If you are experiencing troubles with your son or daughter, it is extremely likely that you're doing one or both of two things.

1. Certainly you are failing to do a job which is rightfully yours: *Making your own life happy.*

2. Very probably you are taking over a job which is rightfully your kid's and not yours: *Running your kid's life.*

The work in this book is aimed to help you change on both of these counts. Because it's easier, we are beginning, in this and the next three chapters, with the second item, coaching you on getting out of running the kid's life. We'll go into much more detail, but now, as a beginning, to get you into a more comfortable situation while you're working on the total problem, we ask you to take the following steps.

Step One

Sit down with paper and pencil and make a list, as complete as you can, of all the things your kid does that bother you.

Even if there is someone else working on this problem with you, do the list and everything else in the book on your own, as an individual. If two parents are working on the problem together, each should make a separate list, and they will probably turn out to have at least some different items.

This list will be the basis of your work in this book, and we hope to coach you to do something about every item.

Once you get underway, you may be able to list eight or ten or more items. Here are sample items other parents have listed:

Things Kids Do that Bother Parents

Stays up late.
-Lies, e.g.:
 Says she is going one place but goes somewhere else.
 Says he did his homework when he didn't.
 Says she didn't steal from my purse.
-Leaves messes in the kitchen.
 Slides the breadboard in with crumbs still on it.
 Leaves wet towels all over the bathroom.
 Leaves dirty dishes in the family room.
 Doesn't feed his pets.
 Doesn't clean up her dog's messes.
-Uses my clothes without asking.
 Dresses like a tramp.
 Uses too much make-up.
 Gives my clothes (hair dryer, cosmetics) away to her friends.

Sneaks out the window at night.
Stays out late or even all night.
Leaves his bicycle (skates, etc.) outside to be stolen.
Leaves my tools outside to get rusty, or loses them.
Ties up the phone for hours.
Runs up large long distance phone bills without asking me.
Won't change clothes after school.
Has a bad attitude, belligerent.
Has a sullen attitude.
Goes with undesirable friends.
Has an older boy friend (or girl friend).
Watches too much TV.
Lies around all day just listening to stereo or watching
    television.
Doesn't do his homework.
Won't go to school.
Is failing in school.
Brings kids in the house while I'm gone.
Lets other kids in who steal from us.
Doesn't take baths.
Won't do chores.
Has tantrums and makes threats when doesn't get his way.
Won't clean up her room. Keeps it a mess.
Runs away.
Fights with brothers or sisters.
Says I don't love her.
Swears.
Calls me names.
Won't do things with the family.
Wants to be by herself most of the time.
Demands money.
Tells others that I mistreat her.
Steals from me or others in family (money, jewelry, coin
    collections, liquor).
Smokes.
Drinks beer with friends.
Smokes pot.
Has pot in his bedroom.
Is sexually active and even promiscuous.
Threatens bodily harm to me or others.
Got his girlfriend pregnant.
Had an abortion, and now is pregnant again.
Knocks holes in the plaster when angry.

Takes someone else's car and goes "joyriding."
Breaks into neighbor's house and steals things.
Goes shoplifting.
Threatens to kill himself.
Rides in cars driven by irresponsible friends.
Is hurting my relationship with my partner.

This is a dismaying list to read. If you'd read it before deciding to have kids it might have influenced you to change your mind. There's a positive aspect to reading it though: you probably don't have all the problems on the list! We still think each of these problems can be seen as an opportunity around which you can change your life for the better rather than merely as a painful hassle. Let's begin now to sort out and bring some kind of order to your list.

Step Two

When your list is made, go over it and pull out for a separate "pile" all the things your kid does which, although they may have consequences for his or her life, will not affect your future life. We will call this the kid's-life pile.

Spend some time on this, thinking about each item as you go along. As you check over your list, you will probably find that some items clearly affect only your kid and thus belong on the kid's-life pile; others clearly have consequences for your life and so do not belong on this pile. Still others you may have to break up into several pieces to find a part that affects you and a part that doesn't.

If you really get stuck deciding whether an item should go on this pile, ask yourself whether you have any direct power over this situation, or not. For example, if the cosmetics you lend your daughter tend not to come back, you could stop lending. However, if she is in the habit of smoking cigarettes while out of the house, there's no direct action you can take to change it. In the first instance you have some direct power over the situation; in the second you don't. We find that items which do not affect your life tend to be things you can't do anything about anyway. We think it's poor tactics to make your stand in an area in which you're helpless to start with, and so suggest that if you can, you put these items on the kid's-life pile. Reserve your strength for areas we'll deal with later in the book in which you do have some leverage.

Of course, the way you select these items will depend on your unique situation; only you can decide whether or not a given item belongs on this pile of things that do not affect your life. Nonetheless, we can go over the list of examples above and suggest items that, by and large, might reasonably go on this pile.

The following items are generally best put on the kid's-life pile, reserving out the rather small portions of them that do affect you and also fall under your control:

- *Stays up late.*

Parents often worry about this item on the grounds that the kid needs his or her rest in order to be ready to get up on time and be fresh for school the next day. It's true that staying up late may have this kind of consequences *for your kid's life*—bleary eyes and drowsiness the next day, perhaps—and this pretty clearly doesn't affect your life. Consider putting this on the kid's-life pile, then, and reserve such aspects as the following, which do affect your life.

Is grumpy the next day.

Prevents me from having privacy and/or a quiet time at night.

Demands I wake him or her next morning.

- *Watches too much TV.*

We can think of consequences for your kid's life here, probably the same ones you have worried about. The kid is probably wasting time; posture and use of the eyes is probably not the best, and the kid is allowing his or her mind to be filled with trivia instead of learning to enjoy using it creatively. None of this affects your life, so this item is probably for the kid's-life pile, with possible reservations like these:

Prevents me from watching my own programs.

Runs TV so long and so loud that the noise bothers me.

● *Doesn't take baths.*

A horrible picture haunts parents whose kids won't wash: You're walking down the street with your kid thirty years from now, you neat and polished, he or she an unwashed, scruffy, and hangdog adult. Everyone you know sees you together and thinks, "Something is terribly wrong with this parent, to let his or her child grow up to be such a slob."

Outside of such shame, your kid's not-washing probably does not affect your life, although it does have consequences for the kid, whose friends, teachers, relatives, etc., develop an opinion of him based on his state of washedness, and probably treat him accordingly. Consider putting this item on the kid's-life list and reserve aspects like this if they are a problem:

She smells, a stale sweaty smell every time she moves.

He gets the furniture dirty when he sits on it.

When it's his turn to cook he doesn't wash his hands, and I have the feeling the food's dirty.

● *Doesn't take care of personal belongings.*

● *Leaves bicycle out where it can get rained on or stolen.*

Almost any adult who has worked to support him or herself feels uncomfortable at seeing valuable things mistreated, and when they're things you have worked to pay for, the discomfort can be acute. Seeing the things you provided being treated cavalierly, you begin to feel unappreciated too. You may develop anxious and resentful feelings about money, also. You've paid for something that is not being valued, and you may feel you're going to have to go on paying for more things, that your money could just dissipate like water going down a sink.

To change the situation around and get yourself back in control of your own financial outgo, we recommend making a distinction between things that belong to your kid and things that belong to you, and put the way the kid takes care of his or her own things firmly on the kid's-life list. It's pretty clear that the loss of your kid's bike, ruining or soiling of your kid's school clothes, the giving away of your kid's money, is going to affect his or her life, and not yours. At the same time, reserve aspects of this item that certainly do have consequences for you.

Expects me to replace lost or ruined or given-away things.

● *Fights with brothers and/or sisters.*

This is one of the most common, surefire worries for many parents with more than one kid, and it takes so many forms and occurs in so many different intensities that we are still being presented with new variations. Each time a new one comes up we tend to think, "This situation really is an exception," and begin to work on it in a different way. Over and over we are brought back to seeing it in the way we describe in this book.

Your major concern when kids fight may be for their safety; you're afraid one will seriously hurt the other. Clearly this would have grave consequences for both hurt and hurter. Even if the outcome is not this drastic, you may fear they are developing life attitudes through the fighting, one learning to be a bully, the other to be a victim. These are serious consequences—and they affect primarily the kids' lives. We suggest that if the kids involved are old enough to run and to tattle, you put this item on the kid's-life pile, keeping out aspects that do affect you directly.

I'm frightened by the possibility of real injury.

They make so much commotion—and I can hear the screaming, noise of scuffling, banging furniture—while they're fighting.

They are so noisy that the landlord threatened eviction.

● *Screams, has tantrums, when doesn't get his or her way.*

You don't like your kid to be displeased or angry with you, and you don't like neighbors or anyone else to know that this exaggerated behavior is going on. Yet, tantrums probably don't have real consequences for your life. For the kid we've known the screaming fits to result in a sore throat and hoarseness, feelings of helplessness at not being able to get what he or she wanted in a more appropriate way, and, sometimes, the exhilaration that comes from exploding once in a while. This is thus probably a kid's-life item.

Some kids throw things when they're angry; it seems to us that whether this should go on the kid's-life pile or not depends on whose things get thrown or get hit by the missiles. If they're your things, it certainly affects your life. If they're his or hers, it seems to us the loss if they are broken is the kid's, not yours, and we'd put the item on the kid's-life pile.

Tantrums are not simple. They are usually in reaction to something you have done and that something could involve either a kid's-life item ("No, you can't go to Jan's until your homework is done") or a parent's-life item ("No, I won't let you take my car tonight"). Tantrums occur too when there is a history of your giving in to your kid. In effect you may have trained your kid to have tantrums by occasionally rewarding them. Now you must retrain him or her. We'll show you how in later chapters.

An aspect of tantrums which might be appropriate for your own pile is the noise. One mother we worked with had a real medical problem with her eardrum. Thus, for tantrums, perhaps you would want to reserve the following:

The noise annoys or pains me.

● *Leaves his or her room a mess.*

This one can rankle some parents almost unbearably, especially mothers. Yet in most cases it affects mostly the kid's life; it is your son or daughter who must live in a pig sty atmosphere, feel ashamed to invite friends in, be unable to find things in the general disorder, perhaps have to wear unwashed and rumpled clothes.

Parents sometimes feel that it is part of their job to train their children to be neat, and that an important element of that training is to insist on a neat bedroom. We'd like to convince you somehow that this is best made a kid's-life item. If you had a boarder who was paying to rent the room, would you be insisting that he or she keep it neat? We think probably not; if a person is paying for the room it's really his or her territory. Of course, your kid is not paying for the room but it seems reasonable that some part of the house be set aside as really his or her territory. Put the cleanliness of your kid's room on the kid's-life pile if you can.

A messy room would seem to affect you only in ways like these:

Leaves door open so I can't avoid seeing the mess.

Runs us out of dishes by leaving them in his room.

Draws ants and mice into the house by leaving smelly food scraps.

Leaves room messy while we're trying to sell the house and want to show it to prospective buyers.

- *Won't do things with the family.*
- *Wants to be by herself most of the time.*

Parents tend to feel hurt, unwanted, rejected, when kids decline to go on family outings and seem to prefer being with friends or alone with a stereo. We'll describe later some things you can do to increase chances of your kid's wanting to go out with you, and here merely suggest that if you can, you put this one on the kid's-life pile. Try thinking of it this way: that you are an interesting, caring, fun person to be with, and if the kid does not choose to be with you, it is his or her loss rather than yours. Aspects you might hold in reserve if they obtain are:

> Prevents me from going out by refusing to accompany me, because I know he will wreck the house, bring other people into the house, and so on, while I'm gone.

> Notifies me she isn't coming too late for me to be able to cancel reservations or make other arrangements.

- *Goes with "undesirable" friends. The sorts of friends who may fall into this category for you are friends who clearly have values different from yours, or who are much older or who have been in trouble with police or who are into sexual activities, drugs, truancy, and so on.*

"To be allowed to pick my own friends" is probably the second most common and urgent thing the teenagers we have seen say they want. The first thing is "more freedom," and even that often turns out to mean "freedom to be with friends of my choice." At the same time we know that good parents are often geared to feel responsible for the kinds of people their kids associate with, and school authorities and counselors sometimes reinforce this responsibility. We've heard a police officer tell the parents, "You're responsible for the people your kid goes around with." However, this is also an item over which you have no direct control, and it doesn't affect your life directly.

In our view, this item is an especially good one for you to use to gain increased freedom for yourself and at the same time make points with your son or daughter. We think it belongs squarely on the kid's-life list. Hold out for further consideration aspects of this item that do affect you, such as:

Brings these "undesirable" friends home against my wishes.

Allows these friends to steal from me.

Has these friends in the house when I'm out.

Demands that I perform services for these friends (driving them to entertainments, and so on).

● *Runs away.*

The first time a kid runs away can be a truly agonizing time for the parent. You will probably experience a real pain and inner pressure––a pain that distracts you from thinking of anything else for some time, a pressure of continual worry, hurt, shame. As long as your son or daughter is out, you will see him or her in every kid you pass who looks anything like yours, and feel a pang every time. Nonetheless, we cannot say that it is the kid who is bringing about all this painful feeling. Rather, it is something we parents do to ourselves on the occasion of a runaway, partly because we believe we should be able to control all of our children's behavior and this action of theirs uncontrolled by us jars that belief, and hurts.

In a typical runaway situation, both kid and parent see it as something the kid is doing to the parent or parents, usually to try to get something (attention if nothing else). To give it some drama and to justify a basically irrational action, they often portray their parents, to any willing ears they can find, as five-horned, web-footed monsters, and the parents are likely to learn of this somehow in the process of the runaway. All of this can make it difficult to put running away on the kid's-life pile. Nevertheless we believe that this is the most effective place for it.

If we look at the kid as an individual responsible for his or her own life in the world, we can view the running away not as something done to the parents but as something the kid does with his or her own life, which affects that life. To the kid belong the dangers, the excitements, the freedom of being out, the knowledge that he or she is being unfair to you, the problem of falling behind or out of school, the job of finding friends who will put him or her up, the discomforts of having to spend a few nights in church gardens, in orchards, on the roofs of supermarkets, and so on. In some states running away is against the law, and this, too, is the kid's offense. If you are providing an adequate home (and we believe that you are or you would not be reading this book), *you* are not breaking the law.

We'd recommend, then, that you put this item on the kid's-life pile. Hold out aspects of the runaway that could directly affect your life.

> Leaves me legally and financially responsible for damages he or she might incur. (However, this also holds when your kid is not a runaway).

> Leaves me not knowing whether to continue to provide a room, groceries, etc.

● *Rides in cars or on motorcycles with irresponsible friends.*

Here your main concern is for your kid's safety. You're envisioning him or her badly injured or perhaps somehow responsible for others being injured. Certainly this item could have tremendous consequences for the kid's future life, and it's also something you can do very little about. If you forbade it, your kid would have the ability to do it behind your back, and you would have lost even that small bit of control over the problem.

Therefore, we think this item belongs on his or her

life list. An aspect you may also be worried about and which would affect you directly is:

Being injured and becoming incapacitated and a burden, incurring hospital costs that I would pay.

● *Drinks, smokes, uses pot or other drugs.*

These activities may be harmful to health as well as illegal, so they certainly have consequences for your kid's life. Aspects that affect your life could be:

Coming home drunk or stoned.

Keeping drug or liquor supplies in the house (this may make you liable for breaking the law).

Police involvement which requires a parental court appearance.

● *Is sexually active.*

As long as your son's or daughter's sexual activity takes place away from where you are, it would seem to affect your life only in quite circumscribed ways, while it has many possible repercussions for him or her. Issues of self image, relationships with other persons, morality, love, possible pregnancy, and venereal disease all enter in and are certainly important decisions for the kid. If pregnancy occurs, even the decision about whether to raise the baby, give it up for adoption, or have an abortion belongs to the young mother in most states. You are not legally responsible to care for the baby or even for your daughter once she has a child. She herself becomes legally adult and responsible for herself and her child when that happens.

Aspects that do affect you are things like the following:

Having sex in our house.

Expecting me to raise the baby.

- *Stays out late.*

- *Sneaks out the window at night.*

Again, your main concern here may be for your kid's safety. You think of all the dangerous things that can happen late at night—muggings, rapes, and so on—and you want your kid to be safe at home. Your son's or daughter's safety certainly is an important factor in his or her life, and affects your life mainly insofar as you worry about it. If you can do so, put this one on the kid's-life list and reserve any aspects of it that do have an effect on your life, such as:

Disturbs my rest by coming in noisily or by waking me up late at night.

Breaks window or door locks coming in or out, and mars walls and furniture by clambering over them.

Puts house open to possible break-in by leaving it unlocked.

- *Wears revealing halters.*

- *Wears scruffy looking clothes.*

- *Uses too much make-up*

The way a kid dresses affects his or her life in many ways: in one sense it's a statement of how the kid sees him or herself to be, or wants to be, and it gives the outside world advance notice of what to expect of him or her. It doesn't affect your life; your way of dressing does that. Further, you have very little real control over how your kid dresses except when he or she is right under your thumb. We'd suggest putting this one on the kid's-life pile, and reserve any aspects that do affect you, such as:

Expects to go places with me, looking like a bum, a streetwalker, etc.

- *Drives a friend's car without a license (or steals a car and goes "joyriding").*

- *Breaks into neighbor's houses and steals things.*

- *Shoplifts at the local department store.*

Certainly these illegal activities will affect your kid's life. He or she is violating other people's rights and at the worst may do something to injure others. The kid is also learning about the law, probably first that it's easy to flaunt it, and then, if he or she is lucky, that it isn't so easy, that it can have very uncomfortable consequences. You cannot directly stop your kid from doing these things, but if they keep up, hopefully the police will intervene before they go much further. At that point your kid may do a great deal of growing up—if you let it be his or her problem.

Sometimes parents hesitate to let the authorities discipline their kids for lawbreaking because they think of being arrested as such a final, drastic event, and because they think that a "record" can be damaging to a person later in life. Even if it were that bad we'd recommend putting this item on your kid's-life list, but it may be reassuring to you to know that a brush with the law is not usually that final nor drastic; most juvenile authorities are for the kids, not against them, and do everything they can think of to get them back into regular life without scars or permanent damage. In some states any record of misdemeanors incurred by a minor can be completely expunged when he or she reaches eighteen. If your kid is experimenting with illegal activities, an encounter with the law without being bailed out by you may be the only thing that will save him or her. It would seem far better to undergo it now than after eighteen. Adult jail is less comfortable, less helpful, and more incriminating than Juvenile Hall.

In short, we suggest you put these items on the kid's-life list. Aspects of these behaviors that you might hold out from this pile because they do affect you are:

Having stolen goods in my house.

Receiving calls from the police.

Going to court with my kid.

Being billed for room and board at Juvènile Hall.

Being billed for damages done by my kid.

- *Won't do homework.*
- *Won't go to school.*
- *Is failing school.*

What your kid does about school certainly has an effect on his or her life—on what kinds of choices will be available in later days, the kind of work your kid will do, the people he or she will mingle with, his or her self image. It is not basically a matter that affects your life; presumably you have already gone through whatever high school grades you want, and have no need to repeat them through your kid. Also, you probably can't make your kid go to school or perform well in it. We haven't even seen it work to "make" kids do their homework. Thus, these school items might well go on the list of things that concern your kid only. Aspects of them you might hold out if they bother you are:

Letting me get phone calls from school authorities who blame me for my kid's misbehavior.

Hanging around the house during school hours.

Living in the home as a freeloader, not carrying his or her weight. (In a sense, your basic deal with the kid is probably that you provide the wherewithal for life support, and the kid get him or herself educated for adulthood. If he or she stops the education and still expects the support without substituting some other contribution, that's freeloading.)

- *Lies around all day just munching out and watching TV.*

This item doesn't sound like much, but it can be a constant irritant to a parent. It's often especially painful because the parent can't think of any good reason for not wanting the kid to lounge about, and thus must cope with feeling unreasonable and guilty as well as frantically annoyed.

In our experience this item is usually a secondary problem. The parent is usually feeling angry and helpless about other items and therefore has a hard time feeling good about anything the kid does. If you feel taken advantage of, rejected, unfairly treated by someone, you are likely to have a negative reaction to everything about that person. Once those more basic problems are taken care of, it becomes easy to feel good about having that person around. We recommend working on those other, more basic items, and putting this one firmly on the kid's-life list, reserving aspects that do affect your life:

Eats up all the groceries.

Litters the place with dirty dishes and cigarette butts.

Prevents me from ever having any privacy.

This list may be enough to give you an idea of what kinds of items appropriately go on the kid's-life list.

There's a whole other group of problems that would seem to be kid's-life items but which we have nonetheless held out of that list. These are the items centering around things your kid *says* or the *attitude* he or she expresses. In a sense, your kid's lying, calling you names, or having a sullen or gloomy attitude need not affect your life unless you take it seriously. However, these items are not so appropriately handled through the approach we're going to recommend for the other items on this pile, and so we will not include them there, but will deal with them separately, later in the book.

The rest of the items remaining on our list (pages 16–18) can be seen to affect you directly, and will therefore be left on your original list as parent's-life items to be dealt with in the second half of this book.

Step Three

You now have a separate pile of things your kid does that really do not affect your life. We're going to ask you to deal with these items in a certain, specific way which we will detail for you in the next paragraphs. However, *please do not carry out those instructions yet.* We recommend the following:

— Read through all of the instructions in the rest of this chapter.

— Then read through Chapters 3 and 4. They will help you develop a rationale for the way you interact with your kid and give you a reservoir of confidence on which to base those interactions.

— Reread the instructions that follow in this chapter, carrying them out this time.

Basically, we're going to ask you to do two things about the items on the kid's-life list. First, *drop the responsibility for these items.* Second, *develop a trust that your kid can and will make the right decisions in these matters for him or herself, and let the kid know you have that trust.*

You may find it fairly easy to do this, and if so, this one procedure can make a noticeable difference in the problems you're experiencing with your son or daughter. However, many parents find this step extremely difficult, and you may be one of them. If so, take it slowly, at your own pace. We don't want you to give up items too fast or too grudgingly, because if you have to force yourself too much you may give them up without letting go the worry and resentment connected with them; that is, you won't be able truly to give them up at all. On the other hand, it's worthwhile to push yourself a little bit; the sooner you really give your kid an item or two the sooner you will feel the relief and the benefits from it and the better you will feel about advancing even further.

Here is how you might go about letting these items go and learning to trust your kid:

FIRST: Pick out the biggest item you can let go of with any ease at all.

NEXT: Take a few minutes to practice giving it up in imagination first. Relax in whatever way helps you feel at peace with the world, and then go through the following sequence in imagination a few times:

Imagine that you see your kid doing this particular thing. As you do, you experience that old, familiar pang— a combination of worry, anger, and the helpless realization that, "I've got to do something about that—and there's nothing I can do that will be effective."

Then imagine that you remember that the responsibility for this behavior is now going to be *not yours but the kid's*, and that you do not have to experience that pang any longer.

A feeling of relief and freedom from having had a weight taken off your back flows through you.

In that relief and freedom, if you feel like it, allow yourself to feel a new interest and curiosity in what the kid might be doing—without your having to feel responsible for it. Let it be as though you were reading a book you like very much and that you know has a happy ending, but you have no idea what the next paragraph will be. With the security of the known happy ending, you can enjoy being surprised. When you can feel a friendly interest, imagine that you turn to your kid and see that he or she is doing this thing from your kid's-life list. You notice this *with interest* and a basic feeling of trust that he or she will be able to work out the problem.

NOW: Rehearse a statement to your son or daughter in which you give him or her the responsibility for this item. It could go something like this:

"Matt, I've been feeling worried and angry about your

not going to school lately, and I've been trying to make you go.

"I've been thinking about it, and now I realize that's silly. I can't make you do anything, and besides it is your life that's affected, so it's really your business.

"I've realized you're quite able to make the right decisions about your school.

"From now on I'm going to stay out of your school decisions and trust that whatever you decide about school is right for you.

"I'm still interested and I'll do my best to help in any reasonable way, if you ask me, but basically, from now on it's your show."

You may notice that this message has only six sentences, that "I" is the subject of every sentence, and that there are no questions in the message. We call sentences of this sort *I-statements*. We'll talk more about effective speech patterns later in the book, and at this point simply ask you to follow suit as much as you can—make it a statement of what *you* feel and are going to do, not a telling your son or daughter what he or she could or should do. *Put what you have to say in I-statements, make it brief, and ask no questions* (such as, "Why don't you want to go to school?" "Would you like me to talk to your teacher for you?" "Did you go to school today?" and so on.)

NEXT: Rehearse a brief statement of the reservations you have about this particular item. For example:

"I am going to get out of your school business; at the same time there are some things *I* want.

"I want the house clear of kids during school hours.

"I want to know everyone in the place is carrying his or her reasonable weight. I don't want to support a freeloader."

Notice again that this message is brief, and it is made up entirely of I-statements. It tells what *you* feel, what *you* want, what *you* are going to do. Make yours clear and short.

Practice your statement until you're quite comfortable

with it.

NOW: Go to your son or daughter and tell him or her openly and directly that you have reached a decision about this particular item and what it is.

THEN: Within the next few days or weeks, give him or her responsibility in a similar way for the remaining items on your kid's-life list.

You may get a surprising response from your son or daughter when you say all this. We've seen kids respond with everything from joy to tantrums, from accusations ("You don't care!") to exhortations to take back the responsibility to apparent apathy and no discernible response. We recommend that you listen quietly to whatever your kid says or does in response to your statement, and reiterate gently that this is what you want to do. Focus your attention not so much on the kid's reaction as on your own resolve to stick with I-statements, to ask no questions, and to make it brief.

Parents too express a wide range of reactions to the very idea of doing what we suggest in this chapter. Some experience an immediate relief. Many others exclaim incredulously, "Do you mean just let the kid run wild?" "Just let the kid go?" Some express concern about being irresponsible themselves: "That's giving up my job of being a guide," or, "I'm responsible for my kid!" Not infrequently a parent says something like, "If I do that then the kid has won." All of these responses are natural and understandable; they all stem from the parent's sincere attempt to do the best possible job of kid raising. In the next chapter we'll look at why you may have had the reaction you did to the things we've suggested. Here we'll just say that if you do what this chapter recommends, you will have taken a major step toward resolving your problem. We say this regardless of how joyously or angrily or sullenly your kid may have reacted to your statement or how hard or easy it may have been for you to do it. You've taken a first step at taking charge of your problem. Now the job is to follow through, building on this first step.

In Chapter 4 we'll deal with how the situation is likely to develop next and some ways of handling that development.

At this point you may be left with a number of items on your original list—things the kid is doing that *do* affect your life. They're important, and we'll deal with them and with the aspects of the kid's-life items that you held in reserve, in the second half of this book.

Three

Why It Is So Hard to Give

Your Kid Responsibility

In the last chapter we asked you to do what professional therapists call "giving up the control." We know all too well that it may be much harder for you to understand or do this than it is for us to write about it. You may be having a great deal of difficulty even considering letting go the items on your kid's-life pile, and even if you're one of the parents who respond to these ideas with relief, you may be experiencing some doubts about the wisdom of it. What leads to these doubts and makes it so hard to do this?

We think we understand why it can be so difficult and even frightening to consider letting your kid go to make his or her own mistakes. We think it's because you are trying to be a good parent, and have the idea that that means such things as the following:

It's my job to see that my son or daughter turns out in a certain way and behaves a certain way. It's my job, for example, to see that he or she turns out to be honest, considerate of others, willing and able to work for a living, having a good self-image, using his or her potential. It's my job to see that he or she behaves in public, goes to school, eats properly, keeps

37

clean, and so on.

It's my job to guide my kid. His or her job is to follow my directions.

I'm obligated to care for my kid. After all, he or she didn't ask to be born.

If my kid gets into trouble, it's my job to bail him or her out of it.

It's right and proper for me to sacrifice for my kid, because the kid's needs and welfare are more important than mine.

It's my job to ensure my kid's safety; I am the one who should be alert for dangerous situations, and protect my kid from them.

It's my job to protect my kid from suffering—from going through disappointments, mistakes and failures.

A great many parents in the world operate on a set of ideas something like these, and by and large it works; at least, large segments of the population brought up according to these ideas seem to survive and get along ostensibly OK. If you are having trouble with your kid, you are probably a caring and conscientious person who is trying to apply some of these ideas in your family. That's why you are pushing your kid to go to school, deciding he or she shouldn't see certain friends, making sure he or she has lunch money, clean clothes, and combed hair, and all the rest of it. No one knows why these ideas "worked" for so many other parents and kids and may even be working for you and some of your kids and aren't working for you and this particular kid. It may be, though, that you are the lucky ones, that something in you and/or your kid senses that there is something incomplete and therefore wrong about these ideas, and, without understanding it exactly, is pressing, through all this trouble, toward a different way. The very fact that you're having trouble may prove to be an opening for both of you to break through to a freer, more expansive, and much happier way of being, with a rejuvenated set of ideas.

What's wrong with the ideas above—aside from the important fact that they're not working for you? We think that, basically, what's wrong with them is that they are based on some condescending and therefore destructive assumptions about what the kid is and what you are. Over and over these ideas define your kid only as a rather helpless being who cannot run his or her life but needs your direction, your support, the knowledge that you "care," to keep him or her going. There's no mention of the kid as initiating anything or as competent to do his or her own thing. This is a very condescending view of your son or daughter. Meanwhile, these ideas define you not as a person who matters for yourself, but rather only in terms of the kid's behavior; you count only insofar as you're a "good parent." Your identity and value do not depend on anything *you* do, or are, but on what the kid does or is. The kid's identity and value depend not on what he or she thinks or is like, but on how well he or she fits your expectations. Each of you is defined by the other and neither is a self-respecting and self-sufficient individual.

Certainly these assumptions conduce to a low self-image on the part of the kid; he or she is being told, in essence, "You are not able to make good decisions; you are helpless and need another person (Dad and/or Mom) to think for you. Further, you are not responsible for what you do: Dad or Mom is!"

In a very deep sense these ideas break down your self esteem too. First, they set up a task for you at which you can only fail. It's as though on the one hand society said to you, through these ideas, "You are a good person insofar as you are a good parent," and, "A good parent controls his or her kid." Meanwhile, your common sense and the way your kid actually behaves tells you, "I cannot control my kid." Thus the total message is, "I must—and yet I cannot—control this person!" It's not surprising if you end up feeling frustrated, trapped, and believing there's something wrong with you.

When a parent gets stuck in this pattern of thinking he or she may be doing an inappropriate parenting job for kids of this age group. Even though few of us ever had formal training to be parents, we learned to control certain activities of our children for their own good. ("No, you can't go in the street with your three-wheel.") Then, as our children matured, we tended to keep the old, progressively more inappropriate, control habits still in force "for their own good." ("No, you can't see Bill any more after he is released from Juvenile Hall.") Playing in the street could be fatal for a child, whereas, for the adolescent, continuing to associate with Bill probably would not be. In that sense you may be carrying habits of controlling your kid which were appropriate when he or she was a child but which are no longer appropriate.

We are sometimes struck by the contrast between kids who rebel against this kind of parental control and those who don't. Sometimes the non-rebelling kid comes to depend too much on parental decision making and reaches adulthood unprepared to carry on alone.

Ann's parents were extremely upset because of the way Ann (16) rebelled against their orders. She had been an A student but now was getting C's and was interested in boys. The current crisis was precipitated by Ann's rebelling against her parents' orders to give up her job at McDonald's so she could spend more time on homework. Ann's older sister (23) had, according to the parents, been a "perfect" adolescent, never giving them any trouble. However, at 23 she was still living at home, had not been successful in keeping a job very long, wanted only to stay home and clean the house, and had no social life to speak of. As you might imagine, we suggested to the parents that their older daughter might have the more serious problem. By giving in to her parents' control, she missed out on learning to take care of herself.

Thus, continuing the struggle to control your kid's life, according to the ideas given in pages 37 and 38, may be giving you terrible trouble right now if you're failing in this control effort. If you're succeeding in your control, your kid may be missing an opportunity to better learn self-directing.

Now, we're going to describe another philosophy—one that we believe would relieve some of the problems you are having and result in a more positive self image for both you and your son or daughter. It's not a set of ideas to be swallowed whole, but rather a few basic assumptions from which you can develop your own, individual ideas.

When a kid is a baby, he or she needs a certain kind of caring in order simply to survive. A baby must be fed, washed, kept warm. So one kind of love you probably gave your kid in early years was caring for his or her physical welfare.

Very soon, though, a baby begins to outgrow these physical needs—becomes able to crawl and then to walk, to feed, dress and wash him or herself, becomes able to take some responsibility for self and for the family project. The small child's physical needs must still be provided for for a long time, but the need for this kind of caring diminishes steadily and is essentially outgrown by the teenage years and indeed, in some societies, by much earlier. We think that ideally you, the parent, outgrow your interest in giving it at the same time.

We think of this caring for the kid's physical welfare as being on one level of love.

There is a second kind of love that the kid and in fact every human being also needs in order to live. It is so essential that babies who do not receive it tend to die young. This is love which wants and cares about the inner being that the person most essentially is, the unique energy or initiative which animates the person. We could say it is love of the other person's *decision-making ability*. From the very beginning, your kid gave out with unique, individual ways of behaving that could have come only from him or her and that, all together, go to make up a totally unique person that you could never mistake for anyone else. Not only does he or she have a unique set of genes, not only is he or she physically unique, with unique finger-prints, but he or she has a completely individual way of doing things. He or she continually makes decisions that you could not predict, that could surprise you—decisions about what friends to make, what foods to prefer, what thoughts to think, and so on. *These individual responses are what you could most naturally love and enjoy about your kid.* You miss out on them when you focus on what your kid is doing that he or she "shouldn't" do, or what he or she is not doing that "should" be done. These individual responses come from a person's own inner being, the part that makes him or her a unique person. They are what tells us a person is alive rather than a doll or robot, and so your enjoyment of them can be called, "enjoying the signs of life."

This enjoyment and wanting of another person's unique way of doing things and making decisions is what we mean by a higher level of love.

Giving your kid this kind of love is the most important thing you can do for him or her. You have already been doing it at some level for many years. No matter how negative you may be feeling toward your kid right now, you could not be having any relationship with him or her at all if there were not at base a core of caring about each other as persons. But this kind of love can also be nearly covered over by other ways of thinking or acting, mostly dutiful ones. Therefore we will talk about how you can give this kind of love to your kid.

Basically, there are two ways in which to communicate this love, and they are both essential in getting you and your kid out of your trouble. One way is what we call *modelling*; it involves letting your kid see that you love and take care of your own inner being. We will talk about it in Chapters 5 through 9. The other is *actively wanting and encouraging your kid's unique decision-making ability.* It's very probable that some of the things you do now which you mean to be helpful to your kid actually function to be-little and block this ability. We ask you to switch your way of thinking around so that everything you do is directed to encourage and open ways for your kid's decision-making ability. If you do that you will automatically be helpful to him or her at all other levels as well.

This is the main point we want to make in this chapter: that you may have been letting yourself feel good about your kid only to the extent that he or she meets the standards of society; that insofar as this is so, you and the kid are both being cheated; that you can learn, instead, to feel good about your kid's unique decision-making ability.

Three distinct steps you can take in this direction right now are:

1. Notice and begin to drop any habit you have of making your kid's decisions for him or her.

2. Learn to enjoy your kid's decision making.

3. Change some of your thoughts and beliefs about your kid.

The work we suggest in Chapter 2 in which you give your kid responsibility for the "kid's-life" items gives you a good, basic start on the first step.

The second step, enjoying his or her decision-making more, has benefits for both you and your kid. A person's inner being expands and develops when he or she is around people who treasure it and enjoy seeing it operate. You can give this to your kid by realizing that here's a living, kicking piece of the Big Show right here in your life, and you have a precious but fleeting opportunity to see it and learn from it and enjoy the show. It will take practice before you can get any enjoyment at all out of the upsetting decisions your kid is making now, but if you drop the feeling that you are responsible for them, you may find yourself freer to notice the pathos and humor and humanness of the situation. A little piece of you may already be doing this; at the back of your mind there may sometimes be a twinge of surprise and amusement at the way your kid is doing things, a little feeling of being touched by the naive and bumbling way he or she is trying to find a place in the world, and a sense of how human and incongruous and vulnerable it all is. These feelings are your response to the touch of life and any little bit of them you experience is to be savored and enjoyed.

A sense of perspective helps in learning to enjoy your kid in this way. You might back up and recall some naive and bumbling things you yourself did when you were your kid's age. Or imagine that it's a neighbor kid who's acting the way your kid is, and you are on the sidelines watching. Neighbors and other adults often get more enjoyment out of kids and are better able to talk with them than the parents, and it seems to be precisely because neighbors do not feel responsible to make the kids' decisions. If the kid is wearing scruffy clothes or spends hours watching television, the neighbor can simply notice this and marvel at the way the world goes—without telling the kid, "You should wear more decent clothes," etc. Why shouldn't a parent take a similar attitude and become more free to enjoy his or her own kid?

Without knowing it you may have been approaching your kid always with the thought, "She should be doing such and so; I'll see whether she's doing what she should," and "I will approve or disapprove of what she's doing." If you would like to enjoy your kid more, try substituting the thought, "I wonder what she's up to now?" with a very free feeling of curiosity and that you need not approve nor disapprove but can simply enjoy, as if you were watching a show. You will find that your kid is surprising—and that one of the great rewards of being a parent is being able to enjoy these constant surprises. You will also find that sometimes you know more than your kid does and can very well see that he or she is heading for some painful consequences, while the best thing you can do is simply state your apprehension and then let those consequences happen. In a way you're in the position of someone watching a caterpillar trying to get out of its cocoon. As a matter of fact, a real caterpillar has to struggle its own way out of the cocoon and in that sense "suffer" if it is to be strong enough to beat its wings and fly; if it is "helped" out of the cocoon it soon dies. Knowing this, an understanding parent can see a son or daughter make decisions that will obviously lead to pain, can let those decisions stand, and can still appreciate and enjoy the humanness, the inevitableness, and the sense of potential and new birth about the situation.

In short, for this step we want you to allow yourself to enjoy your kid's aliveness and unpredictability, even when the thing he or she surprises you with only dismays you at first.

If you'd like more specific instructions on how to enjoy your kid, try these exercises:

List for yourself ten things your kid has done lately that are surprising or unexpected. Now figure out for each one some aspect of the way the kid did it that can give you a sense of pathos and amusement. Find some aspect of each incident that shows how naive your kid can be, or which reminds you of something you did in the past, or which is so much your kid's way of doing things that you recognize him or her in it. Find an aspect of which you can think, "I understand why she did that!"

If you have difficulty thinking of these items, begin now to predict what your kid will do and say for the next five minutes at a time. Say something to your kid, such as "I'm really interested in what is going on in your life" and see whether you were able to predict what his or her response would be. If you were able to predict accurately, enjoy the fact that you were right. If you weren't, enjoy the unpredictability and surprise of it!

Think of some things about which your kid has been eager. Notice whether you get a little feeling of understanding and of wanting to see the kid get what he or she wants when you think of these things. This feeling, of wanting the kid to have or be or do what he or she wants is a little piece of the love and enjoyment we're talking about.

The third step you can take to communicate love to your kid, changing your thoughts and beliefs in a positive direction, is vitally important because of the powerful way in which people's beliefs interact with their actions. Without being aware of it, *we inevitably act toward making our inner beliefs come true.* Thus if you believe your kid (or yourself) to be bad, helpless, or sneaky, you will also, without being aware of it, act to influence your kid (or yourself) to be just that. On the other hand, if you believe him or her to be basically good, to be able to make good decisions, and to be quite capable of running his or her life, you will inevitably and without effort influence the kid in this direction. Even if you never say a word about it, your kid picks up your belief about him or her from the way you act, and because you are the parent, tends to take it seriously and to make it his or her belief as well. Then he or she begins acting to make it come true.

At this point you may be saying, "But my kid *is* doing these wrong things, making bad decisions right now. How can I change my view of that?"

Decisions generally have, from the decider's viewpoint, both good and bad consequences, some of which occur shortly after the decision is made, others which occur later. The more mature and experienced a person is, the more he or she pays attention to the longer range consequences. Thus adolescents tend to focus on the short term consequences while parents give greater consideration to the longer term consequences. This is in fact the source of much parent-adolescent conflict.

When a parent forces or tries to force a kid to decide in a certain way, the parent is generally focussing less on short term consequences and more on intermediate term consequences of the decision. However, there is an even longer term consequence that both parent and kid are ignoring, namely, *the learning, by the kid, to see all the consequences of a decision and to take them into account.* By learning to trust his kid to make effective decisions, the parent achieves both the short term advantage of a conflict-free relationship with the kid, and the longer range benefit of seeing his or her kid learn to see more clearly and to take account of longer term consequences of decisions. When the parent prevents (or tries to prevent) the kid from making a decision that has painful longer term consequences, the kid has fewer opportunities to experience the negative consequences and even when he or she does, pays them little attention because of being so focussed on fighting the parent's control.

Thus, having faith in your kid's ability to make good decisions can act to enhance his or her ability to do so. And your previous judgments about your kid's decisions may have been too narrow, considering your over-all wants for your kid. For example, your daughter's decision to go shoplifting may have consequences which influence her later decision to be a person who doesn't steal, so that viewed from a larger perspective, it was a good decision.

We're saying that your underlying beliefs influence what you and your kid think of yourselves and put a limit on what you can do, be, have, in your lives. By changing those beliefs about yourself and your kid, you can substantially influence what's happening in the total situation with him or her.

Here's a list of some beliefs parents often hold about their kids, together with the kinds of reciprocal belief that the kid is likely to develop:

Parent	*Kid*
I am responsible for what my kid does.	Dad (or Mom) is responsible for my actions; I am not responsible for what I do.
He won't make it.	I won't make it.
She can't make decisions.	I can't make decisions.
She's stupid.	I'm stupid.
He's mentally ill.	I'm mentally ill.
She's worthwhile insofar as she's "good"—goes to school, conforms, is clean, polite, dutiful.	I am of worth for the way I fit in with what others want. Decisions I make for myself are not of value.
He can't take care of himself.	I can't take care of myself.

We want you to work on the way you think, and change every one of these to something positive. For example:

Parent	*Kid*
My kid is responsible for what she does.	I'm responsible for my own actions.
He'll make it to whatever situation is best for him.	Of course I'll make it.
She can make decisions.	Of course I can make my own, good decisions.
He's basically OK.	I'm OK.
I can trust him to take care of himself.	I can and I will take care of myself.
I don't know what he'll do next, and it will sure be interesting to see what it is.	Mom's interested in me, and she trusts that I'll make decisions that are right for me.

If you are seriously interested in changing your thinking about your kid from the first list to the second one, here is what we suggest you do.

Supply yourself with a small writing pad or some blank cards and a pen or pencil that you can keep with you for several days. Then, as you go through your day, notice how, every once in a while, you think about the situation with your kid and experience a sort of pang because that situation is such a problem. Every time you get this pang, notice what kind of thought you're having about your kid. Don't be fussy or agonize about it; just notice the first thought that comes to your mind when you think about him or her. It may be something like, "I hate this situation," "Feeling sick about it," "She's getting to me," "This won't work," "There's something wrong with him," or the like. Now get out your pad and pencil and write the thought.

Now write after it a new sentence, beginning with your kid's name, and continuing, "... has everything he or she needs to make his or her own decisions and run his or her own life."

Do this conscientiously for several days, until you notice that this thought pattern is becoming a habit; that is, that every time you feel a pang about the situation with your kid, you're beginning automatically to follow it with the reassuring thought: "My kid has everything he or she needs to make the right decisions and to run his or her own life."

In this chapter we've been trying to make it easier for you to drop the responsibility you may have been carrying for decisions that your kid can make about his or her own life.

Let's make it clear that we are *not* talking about encouraging your kid to walk all over you, nor to disdain the "shoulds" of society. That wouldn't work, if only because it would mean neglecting and even mistreating your own inner being. Neither are we suggesting you ignore your kid or say you don't care ("Go ahead then, see if I care!"). You can go on caring and being interested while refusing to take over any of your kid's decisions.

We are talking about your seeing people as capable decision makers rather than as helpless, and doing everything you can to encourage your kid's making his or her own decisions.

At this point parents often bring up to us a deep concern they have about what might happen if they "let" their kid make his or her own decisions in this way.

Isn't it dangerous?

She might go out and get raped, mugged, even killed.

He doesn't know how to handle himself; he'll get himself into real trouble if I don't guide him.

Their concern is certainly valid. Indeed there are dangers out there in the world, and kids and other people too do get raped, assaulted, even killed, every day. *All the more reason to aim toward making the kid responsible for his or her own behavior as soon as possible.* The only real protection a kid has against these dangers is his or her own common sense and the knowledge that it's up to him or her to watch out for the dangers and make appropriate decisions about them. If the kid has the idea that worrying about dangers and making decisions about them is your job, he or she is likely to leave it to you and enjoy the carefree feeling of not being responsible. This is truly dangerous because the kid can then go out feeling that all sorts of things are safe because you are in the background and will pick up the pieces should there be any trouble. The fact is that you can't always be in the background nor pick up the pieces, so the kid is operating on a very false feeling of security. Thus we think the best thing you can do toward really protecting your kid against dangers is to drop the idea that it's up to you and let the kid know you are counting on his or her ability to make the right decisions for him or herself.

If you have the idea that you should wait to give the kid this responsibility until he or she demonstrates an ability to take it, please reconsider. People do not necessarily learn to be responsible simply by getting older; you may know of people of thirty or forty who still will not take responsibility for their own lives. People learn to be responsible by finding themselves in situations in which they know they're on their own and making decisions for which they take the consequences. By protecting your kid against the dangers of life you may be preventing him or her from developing the very strength it takes to handle them. We find that when kids are really given full trust in their ability to run their lives, the ability to do just that suddenly shows itself in even the most unlikely kid. The lack of faith kids may show in their own ability seems related to lack of faith which others in their environment show to them.

If giving up efforts to control the different aspects of your kid's life is still very difficult for you, we suggest you give up whatever you comfortably can, pushing yourself just a little. Reserve the others for the time being. Perhaps later, as you see the positive results of doing what you can now, you will feel comfortable giving up more. Whatever you can do is likely to give long term benefits to you and your kid.

Four

How Your Kid May Respond

In the last chapter we talked about an attitude of actually *wanting* to see your kid make his or her own decisions. In this chapter let's work on what's likely to happen when you do hand over to your kid the right to run his or her own life.

What is your son or daughter likely to do with this new "freedom" if you decide to move out of the job of making decisions for him or her?

Most of the kids we see say that what they most want is more freedom to run their own lives. Given the urgency of this demand, one might expect that when they get it, they would respond with joyous faces and a happy smile. True, this does happen once in a while, but we have been amazed at how many kids, when their parents finally agree to "let" them make their own decisions, do not look happy at all. They're more likely to look glum, and to say things like, "You don't care about me," "You'll never live up to it," or even (and these are direct quotes): "I'm not sure I'm ready to make my own decisions," and "Please keep checking up on me!" And very often the first thing they actually do with the new freedom is to act even worse than they did before, in what is apparently in part an attempt to get the parents to take the control back.*

Let's see why they should behave in this way.

We think that an important part of every kid really needs and wants "freedom"—wants to and can take charge of his or her life, make responsible decisions, and be his or her own person. *Another part is scared of this freedom, wants to be saved from it, and will do everything possible to get the decisions made somewhere else.*

This is far from just a kid problem; every human being is in this situation, all through life. Right from the start, we all want to "do our own thing," and at the same time want to pull back from it. Everybody wants to stand up and be definite and make his or her own life decisions, and also wants simply to stick with the safe old habits and let somebody else make the decisions. We're all a little like the circus lion in *Don Quixote* who longed to be free from its cage, out in the open plains. One day the cage door was accidentally left open, and the lion leaped out into the open. As soon as it did, however, the weight of all the freedom and responsibility it could now have came over it, and, in the story, it turned and *ran back into the cage.*

We all have the same kind of choice to make that the lion did, many times every day, between doing our own brave new thing and just going along with ready-made decisions. Probably most of us choose sometimes one way, sometimes the other, and most of the time manage a reasonably comfortable balance between these two ways. Generally we aren't even aware that we're constantly making this choice.

However, over and over in our lives, things happen to make us re-think the way we've been choosing. Significant people enter or leave our lives, or we learn new things, or we graduate, or get married, or have children. Every such change is a kind of crisis because it presses us to choose again, either to begin making more of our

---

* It is also in part a "testing" of the parents' seriousness in dropping the control.

own decisions, or to let ourselves be run even more by the outside. It's never settled in a final way, because we keep getting new chances, over and over, to make the choice again.

It's probably clear that the writers of this book favor the decision-making choice over the use-the-ready-made-decisions choice. We think that ideally in human development a person becomes more and more able and willing to take over more and more of his or her own life decisions. That is what, psychologically, we call growing up, maturing, becoming responsible, becoming free, expanding one's consciousness. We know that both ways of choosing are important, and that everyone is inevitably going to make the use-the-ready-made-decisions choice many times, but over the long run hopefully the over-all movement through all the "crises" is toward taking the right to run one's own life.

If you're having trouble with your kid, it's very likely that both of you are in this kind of crisis in which part of you wants very much to use your own head and run your own life, and another part is pressing you to fit in with ideas from outside yourself.

The kid is in this crisis because he or she has reached an age at which, in this society, people begin establishing anew that they really are their own persons. When we look at the kid's situation, we see that up to about age eleven or twelve, he or she has been learning a great many new things, and probably in large part *they've been your idea.* Even a child who objects vigorously all the way through probably learns much by modelling after you, the parent— learns to walk rather than crawl, to speak English, to use fork and spoon rather than fingers, to dress rather than go naked, to go to school, and many other things.

After all this has been learned, there comes a time for the kid to learn a next big thing. This is to realize even more fully that he or she too can originate decisions, that he or she is a person separate from you or anyone else, a person who does run his or her own life. To stay healthy, the kid *has* to realize he or she is not a carbon copy, and that the impetus for his or her actions comes from inside him or herself and not from outside. In other words, it becomes important for the kid to develop an identity of his or her own. To do so, the kid must make some decisions that are different from yours, simply in order to realize he or she *can* originate ideas.

In our society the inner necessity for doing this usually hits kids some time between eleven and sixteen. It's basically a healthy and positive thing and it means the kid is growing and not that he or she hates you or is turning out badly. Later, after the kid has gone through this and realized that of course he or she is a separate person, he or she may come back to you and end up following many of your ideas after all—but will then be doing so because he or she wants to, because it's his or her own idea, as an adult, to do so.*

Now, we want to emphasize what a scary thing this inner pressure to make one's own decisions is for your kid. He or she is in the position of the lion, for whom it was time to step out and make his own decisions, and who was also scared to do so. Certainly a piece of the kid honestly wants and needs to be free—and this is the direction of growth—but there is usually also a kind of panic at the idea of actually being free. The temptation is very great to run back into the cage, and most kids do so many times.

The way kids run back into the cage is by *getting someone else to make decisions for them*. The sequence is something like this:

1. The daring thought occurs to the kid of making a responsible decision of his or her own.

2. A panicky feeling comes over him or her.

---

* It takes a higher level of maturity than most adolescents have to make a decision to do something that is right for them while a parent is insisting that they do *that same thing*. More usually they will "show their independence" by doing the opposite, not realizing that in the process they are actually showing dependence.

3. The kid does something that he or she knows will get to you, *in order to get you to make the decision.*

4. You respond by telling him or her how to behave —supervising, scolding, approving or disapproving, and so on.

If the kid can accomplish this—get you or someone else to say how he or she should behave, to supervise, to approve and disapprove—then the kid does not have to do it. He or she is safe from having to make self-decisions. Now, having set someone else up as the bossy decision maker, the kid can resent being "dictated to," insist loudly upon wanting freedom, and meanwhile do as he or she pleases without having to feel responsible.

Going through this sequence over and over is not as comfortable a position as it may sound like, and the morose and sullen expressions of many of our acting-out teenagers may reflect the way it actually feels. It's an uncomfortable position because the kid can never make it complete. Something in him or her knows it is not meant to live in a cage, simply obeying or defying other people's decisions, that it is meant to be free and make self-decisions, and this something keeps prodding the kid from inside. Things keep coming up that press the kid to consider leaping to freedom again by making a responsible decision. However, this would be like leaping out of the cage; the very thought brings up the panic again, and so the kid quickly puts the idea down. He or she does so by once again provoking you or someone else to take over the controls—doing something that will get you to scold or punish, to approve or disapprove, to question, to supervise, to tell him or her what to do and what not to do. Once you do respond in this way, the kid is safe again, back in the cage—probably unhappy, but at least safe. However, it doesn't last; before long the idea of running his or her own life pops up again. The cycle keeps repeating itself, and the kid has to manipulate you again and again to keep you on his or her back.

Almost always both you and the kid are unaware of operating according to this pattern, and wouldn't know what we were talking about if we asked why you do it. Yet the chances are high that a good bit of this is going on between you.

We could say that the kid has worked him or herself into an addiction to negative attention. Every time the possibility of making his or her own responsible decision comes up, the kid responds by provoking *you* to take the responsibility instead, and you do so by looking at him or her in one way or another with negative attention, which says to the kid, "I say you should do so and so." Without necessarily being aware of it, most kids nevertheless understand very well what things will bother their parents and how to use these things to provoke just the degree of advice, punishment, restriction, or disapproval they're looking for. In one family the kid does it by staying out late or calling the parent names; in another it's by saying the parent doesn't care, or by refusing to take baths. One teenager we knew did it by assuming a very innocent air and then asking her father questions like, "Dad, what do you think about girls who get pregnant?" At that time she had no interest in becoming pregnant, nor was she honestly curious about what her father thought (she already knew), but this kind of question got her just the right amount of startled and upset attention to assure her that her father was still acting as her watchdog and she did not have to be responsible.

In order to stay in the one-down, abused position negative attention provides, kids will not only provoke negative attention from you and from authorities in general; they also make the most of what they do get by exaggerating it, and even invent it wholesale if they have to. Many is the kid who confides to friends the cruelty, strictness, or uncaringness of what the world would consider perfectly reasonable parents; to be able to describe the worst mistreatment becomes a rather glamorous thing to do among teenagers. A kid achieves safety, in the sense we're speaking of here, by setting him or herself up as a desperate, misunderstood character. Since you can't really be a desperate character without a villain, the kid must then provoke whomever he or she can (probably you!) to take the role of forbidding dictator. And once is not enough; the kid must keep on provoking you in order to maintain you and him or herself in these roles. Some of the hassles between you and your kid may have been more basically "about" the kid's attempt to get you to take that forbidding stance again than "about" the issues you thought you were arguing about.

We are suggesting that many of the disturbing things your kid does are done not because they're so much fun nor because the kid hates you but are done *in order to get you to give negative attention and thereby save the kid from having to make his or her own responsible decisions.* In a sense the kid is addicted to negative attention as if to a drug, and you are in the position of supplier. We would go even farther with the analogy and say that the drug is a harmful one; your negative attention actually encourages the kid to continue evading making his or her own responsible life decisions.

In short, what the kid has probably been *getting* at this time in his or her life is negative attention—scolding, disapproval, worried advice, messages of despair at how he or she is turning out, ever more desperate attempts to control him or her. What the kid *needs* in this situation is help and encouragement to make the make-my-own-decisions choice.

You may well have been in something like this pattern with your kid. Now, in this book, we're asking you to drop trying to control the decisions that really belong to your son or daughter. In accord with this pattern, he or she is very likely to respond at first by trying to provoke you into taking the controls back. He or she may do any of the things we've listed on page 2, or may upscale activity in the very areas in which you have just given "freedom", or may come up with some completely original provocative behavior.

We want you to be comfortable about handling such flare-ups, so we ask you to prepare for them ahead of time by studying the recommendations we will make about what you can do if your kid reacts in this way. First, though, realize that the more prepared and relaxed you are about the possibility of getting such reactions, the less intense they are likely to be. In situations in which parents have begun to drop the controls as we're asking you to do in this book, kids do less trying out and provoking of the parents the more sincere and thoroughgoing the parents are in actually dropping the controls. The more firmly you are committed to following through on what you started in Chapter 2, the sooner the kids seem to realize you do mean it, realize you actually want them to take care of themselves, and begin to do so.

Here, then, are some ways you might act if and when your teenager seems to behave worse than ever after you have dropped your control over the kid's-life items.

When you become aware that the behavior that has troubled you is going on, your first reaction may be a flash of anger, disappointment, frustration. If so, STOP— refrain from saying or doing anything about the behavior while you consider the following ideas.

a. Your experiencing this anger, disappointment, or frustration is the first step in giving your kid the negative attention he or she is hooked on but should not have. If you go ahead and express it further it may only reinforce the kid in irresponsible behavior.

b. The kid is not doing anything to *you* in this behavior (Remember, we are still talking only about the kid's-life items). This behavior affects his or her life, but not yours. How about letting the anger, disappointment, and frustration that may go with that behavior be his or hers too? Hearten yourself and get back a long range perspective on the situation.

If it helps you to drop the anger, etc., try imagining that it is an equal age friend or an aunt or uncle of yours who is behaving in this way, instead of your kid. You may find yourself taking it less personally, and feeling sorry, surprised, perhaps concerned, that this other person has this problem—rather than angry or frustrated.

c. It's true that your kid seems to be pushing you to take over control from the outside again, but just as certainly there is a part of him or her that wants and needs to be set free of it. Trust that that part, the aspect of your kid that is very well able to make good decisions, is there ready to take over when all this trouble between you is over.

Whatever your first impulsive feeling about the behavior may be, *stand firm in your decision not to take back the controls*. When the behavior happens, you may feel an immediate urge to respond as you are used to doing—by feeling sorry for the kid, expressing alarm, asking questions, shaking your head, giving advice. DON'T. No doubt you will slip up a few times—perhaps many times —before you completely overcome the habit of trying to control your kid, but start over as many times as you need to until you can do it. Think of your negative attention to your kid as a dangerous drug, and refuse to continue dispensing it.

What to do instead:

Remain friendly and courteous in your manner with your kid. Since you have previously been the supplier of negative attention, it's important that you now supply something very different. The two crucial elements of negative attention are that (1) it's negative, and (2) it's usually highly charged. An attitude that's generally accepting and at the same time relaxed and low key will provide a good antidote. Keep remembering: "I'm doing OK; it's this other person who has a problem," and, "This person has not done anything to me."

Generally, keep your attention focussed on your own activities, so that you are not even alert to notice whether or not the kid is doing these things that affect only him or her. When you do notice that the behavior is happening, do nothing about it until and unless 1) You haven't been able to drop it from your mind and still feel bothered by it, or 2) It is brought to your attention in a very clear way—that is, until your kid tells you about it directly, or does it right in front of you, or someone else—police, school official, neighbor—tells you about it. Do not play detective, ferreting out how your kid is behaving.

When you do get a clear message that behavior that troubles you is happening, talk with your kid if you want to, but do it in a special way—a way in which you keep responsibility for your own behavior while refusing to assume responsibility for the kid's behavior. You can do this by using mostly I-sentences, sentences telling what you think, feel, want, will do, so that in a sense, the focus is on you rather than on your kid.

Here is a sequence of things you might incorporate into what you say to your kid instead of the negative attention responses you used to make. Use any of them that feels right for you.

1. Make clear in one sentence what you're talking about. If the behavior has come to your attention in some way other than your kid's telling you directly, tell him or her what it is.

> The school attendance office called today to say you had not been there for ten days.

> I notice you're riding on your friend's motorcycle with no helmet.

> The police tell me you were picked up for being drunk in public.

2. Tell the kid how you are feeling about this situation— in an I-sentence.

> I am concerned to hear about it.

> I feel sad about this.

> I'm worried when I hear this.

> I'm surprised.

3. Point out any consequences you see.

> It seems to me if you do this, the consequences will be such and so.

If you're quite anxious about the behavior, tell your kid the fantasy you have about what may happen. It's OK to play this up; it may even help you to exaggerate it to absurd lengths. As long as you stay responsible for the fantasy (by presenting it in terms of I—as your thinking) it won't hurt your kid nor provoke him or her into actually fulfilling it.

> I'm imagining you'll quit school and go out on the streets and get raped and not be able to get a job and end up on welfare.

> I'm afraid you'll go out on the motorcycle and get in an accident and be hurt and go to the hospital and have to be operated on and have permanent brain damage and become a vegetable.

4. Acknowledge your helplessness while disclosing what you wish your kid would do.

> I want you to finish high school, and I know I can't control you.

> I'd like to see you in by ten o'clock, and I know I can't make you do anything.

> I'd like to see you decide against pot, although I know I'm helpless to make that decision.

5. If it's appropriate and you really want to, remind your kid once that you're willing to help if he or she wishes. Then, if your kid does ask you to help, make sure you merely give him or her a hand and do not take the situation over. Inquire as to exactly what would be helpful and then confine yourself to it. Let any further ideas come from him or her. If no more help is asked for, stay out of the situation.

6. (And this is a very important step): State your belief that your kid can and will make the right decisions for his or her life.

I know you'll make the right decision for you.

I'm sure you'll come up with a good solution.

I know you've got what it takes to figure it out in the long run.

The total message you might give, then, when you notice your kid doing something that's his or her business and which nonetheless worries you, is something like this:

I see by this notice from the school that you're failing this semester. I feel sorry about that, but I know you'll figure out the best way to handle it for yourself. Let me know if I can help.

I notice you're into marijuana quite a bit. I keep imagining you'll become a burnt out kid and injure your brain and lose the ability to do athletics and schoolwork. I wish you'd quit, although I know I'm helpless to make you do anything. And I know you'll make the right decision, whatever it is, for yourself.

Your kid may do some things that result in outside pressure on you to intervene. For example, neighbors may complain to you about damage done by your son or daughter; school officials may hold you responsible if your kid misbehaves; police may phone you in the middle of the night to tell you that your kid has been arrested and that you should pick him or her up at Juvenile Hall.

In these situations the kid has, in a sense, enlisted society to pressure you into taking over responsibility for him or her. It would be best not to give in even to this pressure. Do what you feel is right for you to do under the circumstances calmly, without yielding to the pressure to scold, blame, question, ignore your kid, or that other pressure, to feel guilty because your kid did something wrong. This will be hard for you, and we do not mean to treat it lightly. It may help to plan in advance what you will do if you get phone calls like this. The way you find out about your kid's misbehavior may catch you by surprise, and it may be helpful to tell yourself in advance, "Whatever happens, I will calmly and deliberately take what seems like the best action without yielding to the pressure to do immediately what someone else seems to want me to do."

If you stay relaxed, it may even be possible to use this kind of situation to advantage, to demonstrate that you do indeed see your kid and not yourself as responsible for his or her actions. When the neighbor calls, for example, try putting your kid on the phone and let him or her work out a way to make things right. If the school authorities report to you that your kid is misbehaving, tell them you give them your full permission to do whatever they do with kids who behave in that way, and simply deliver their message to the kid. If you receive an ominous looking letter from the school addressed "to the parents of" your kid, hand that letter to your kid saying something like, "I believe this is for you, Bob." If the police tell you to collect your son or daughter from Juvenile Hall, arrange to do so when it's convenient for you; don't leap out of your sleep to do it, nor interrupt your working schedule. In these ways you tell the kid that you care enough about him or her as a decision-maker that you are not going to bail him or her out, and the consequences of your kid's own behavior will fall not on you but on his or her competent shoulders.

What should you do if your kid does something extreme that is potentially harmful to him or herself or to others—gets involved in unusually excessive use of alcohol or drugs, makes a serious suicide threat or attempt, or seriously threatens harm to others? This, we think, becomes a special case. When kids do things that could so obviously lead to their being arrested or taken to a hospital, we assume that they need the outside controls more than they need the freedom for the time being—controls firmer than you could give them, that they can't break. The principles we are talking about in this book apply to these kids just as to any others, but we feel that the element of physical danger makes these situations too tricky for you to handle alone. These kids have often already become involved with some kind of authority that can provide a situation with limits—police and probation officers, medical persons, and so on. In these situations we suggest you make the fullest use of what these people can do in the way of setting limits for your kid. Working through the program in this book would be an excellent *additional* approach for you to take in trying to raise kids who do this kind of acting out.

On a short-term basis, then, when you hand over responsibility for personal decisions to your kid, you can expect anything from immediate improvement in the situation to flare ups of even worse behavior than you started with. Don't be afraid of these possible flare ups. If you're ready for them they need not be frightening, and if you're firm and sincere about really turning responsibility for personal decisions over to your kid, they are likely to be brief. When they're over, if you stick to what we have suggested that you do, we think you have every right to look forward to a more rewarding and comfortable situation than you had before.

One last bit of advice to you as you work on applying these ideas with your kid: *Do not give up.* The approach we're suggesting is powerful—more powerful than it may sound at first, and sometimes using it will resolve situations for parents and kids almost immediately. In many other cases it takes longer. You may be one of the parents who sees little or no change either in your kid or in yourself for some time, even though it seems to you that you're doing everything we've talked about. It's important that you stick with it and be alert to instances in which, without realizing it, you are still doing things in the old way. In this approach you're working for a change in a whole life way of looking at things, for you and your kid. You can do a lot to move in the direction of that change by doing all the small things we suggest in this book, but there's also a sense in which you have to grow into it. Also, you and/ or your kid may simply have to go through more hassle, may have to hit bottom, as it were, before the situation begins to reverse. So hold in there and be prepared to be thorough and persistent in applying these ideas. Assume that everything you're doing that we've talked about *is* helping, and that the positive results will accumulate to a reasonably happy ending—whether or not you see benefits immediately. We know from the many desperate parents we've worked with that it can happen.

At this point, if you've read through and thought about this chapter and Chapter 3, and have done the things we have suggested, you're ready to make a formal handing over of the controls for his or her life to your kid. Go back to pages 32 to 35 of Chapter 2 to do this. Then proceed to Chapter 5, in which you begin to lay the groundwork for dealing with the parent's-life items by learning to take back responsibility for your own happiness.

Five

Taking Back Responsibility

for Your Own Life

Let's begin now to prepare for your successful handling of the rest of the items on your list, the parent's-life
items. In this chapter and the next we'll work to help you
develop the basic attitude that will enable you to do that.
It's an attitude we call "taking care of yourself," by which
we mean that you respect, care about, and can be counted
on to be loyal to your own inner self.

If you are experiencing trouble, either because of
something your kid is doing or for some other reason, it
is almost certain that, in one way or another, you have not
been taking care of your own wants and needs. Without being aware of it, you are ignoring a voice from within yourself.

Everyone has a signal giver inside, an inner being
which is constantly sending him or her daring thoughts:

I feel...
I want...
I might...
I can...
I will...
I'm going to...

Ideally, there is a strong, positive relationship between you and this inner signal-giver. You hear it, respect and care for it, and trust it to guide your behavior—and it in turn is trustworthy. It can be seen as your primary task in life, to fulfill this inner being of yours.

However, many of us learn very early in life to ignore, even fear this inner voice. We get so we do not even hear it, and instead develop the habit of focussing on messages from outside ourselves to guide what we do.

Most of the ideas of what a "good parent" does were like this; they came from society, not from yourself, your own common sense.

It's not uncommon for ignoring one's own inner voice to become such a habit that a person becomes able to hear and take care of what other people need, but does not hear nor pay attention to his or her own wants and needs.

A capable executive found that when he was sitting in a restaurant and felt cold because the air conditioner was turned up too high, he felt obliged to endure the chill and say nothing. However, when his wife complained of being cold, he immediately asked the waiter to adjust it—for her.

A young mother shopped for groceries that would fit the likes and dislikes of every individual in the family—except herself. It simply didn't occur to her to consider what she might like or dislike.

You can ignore your own inner voice to such an extent that eventually your mood is determined not by what your own signal-giver wants and decides to feel, but by what other people do and say. Very likely your mood is being determined by your kid right now in the sense that:

If he or she is "good," happy, or is succeeding in school you feel fine.

If he or she misbehaves, or is unhappy, or fails, you feel miserable.

If this is the case, your mood is being determined by a person outside yourself. It is as though you've taken the power to run your own feelings, your own life, which originally is *your* power, and given it to your kid. Now he or she determines your mood and all you can do is feel helpless and perhaps resentful about the way your kid is using this power.

We believe that every time you look outside yourself for direction in this way and ignore your own inner signal giver, you are betraying yourself. If you could be really sensitive to your inner voice, you could hear it crying out with hurt every time you do it. Ideally this inner being has a champion—namely, you—and when you fail to listen to it, it is as though its champion had abandoned it. It is when this has happened that feelings of depression, resentment, frustration arise. People almost always *experience* these uncomfortable feelings as having to do with events in the outside world, such as the misbehavior of one's kids.

I'm depressed because of the way my son is turning out.

I'm frustrated because she just won't go to school.

We believe that in a deeper sense, however, these feelings are always "caused" by a person's betrayal of his or her own signal-giver, which feels more and more desperate and smothered the more its signals are ignored.

It is important, for the work in the rest of the book, to get back in touch with this inner signal-giver, to commit yourself to take care of it and be loyal to it, and give it its rightful place as authority over your behavior. We urge you to get into the habit of taking care of your own wants and needs.

In this chapter we give several specific exercises aimed at helping you learn to pay attention to your inner voice. The first four should be done the first time you read this chapter. The remaining three are to be done when you settle down seriously to prepare yourself to stand up for your own rights.

Exercise One

Think of all the people you are responsible for taking care of. Right now, before reading further, count them on your fingers.

When you have counted all you can think of, stop, and ask yourself this question: Did I include myself in this list?

Many of the parents we see put a great deal of energy into taking care of people, and readily spread their caring anywhere in the world—except toward themselves. Do you see what a put-down that is for one's own inner being?

Exercise Two

To make sure you have yourself firmly on the list of people you are responsible for taking care of, imagine that you suddenly discover you have one more child, a child you have been paying little attention to. This child is your own inner being. Now ask yourself whether you have been giving this child as much of your time, care, and attention as you have the other persons you care about. Is there a sense in which you've been like the stepmother in the fairy tale, treating your inner child as a Cinderella, and favoring other people in the way the stepmother favored the stepsisters?

Resolve that whatever else you may do in your life, from now on you will take care of your own inner being.

Exercise Three

Sit down with paper and pencil and before reading beyond this sentence, write down your answer to this question: "What do I owe my kid?" (Read no further until you have completed your answer).

Now write down your answer to the question: "What does my kid owe me?"

When both questions are answered, compare the two answers. Did you make it a two-way street, so that you

and your kid owe each other approximately even deals? Or
was it lopsided? If it was, do you know any reason why it
"should" be?

Now try out this idea just to see how it fits for you:
"I don't owe my kid anything. My kid doesn't owe me anything. Each of us is a free person, able to run his or her
own life—and free to do for the other what we *want* to
do."

Try out this idea too, to see how it fits for you: "I
do not owe myself to anyone else. I owe myself to me."

Exercise Four

Try out these sentences to see how they feel when
you say them:

I have a right to privacy.

I have a right to be treated with courtesy.

I have a right to be happy.

I have a right to do as I wish with my own time.

Now ask yourself: "Who is responsible for seeing that I
have these rights?"

Try out this sentence: "I owe my inner being these
rights."

It's possible that you may be finding these ideas startling, even shocking. Parents sometimes exclaim to us,
"Isn't it selfish to take care of myself? Immoral? Other
people will disapprove of me, and I will feel guilty." Here
are some of the ways in which we answer these questions.

We are *not* recommending that you become selfish
and ride roughshod over other people. We do ask that you
give your inner being equal rights with the other people
in your life, and that you trust that, far from harming
others, your doing so will actually be beneficial to them,
too. Shakespeare put it well:

This above all: to thine own self be true,
And it must follow, as the night the day,
Thou canst not be false to any man.

You can give to others only if you first have something to give. If you were surrounded by a thousand people
all dying of thirst, and you had an empty bucket, you could
do nothing for them until you filled your bucket. Learning
to be loyal to and take care of your own inner being is
filling your bucket. When you have done that, you can then
take better care of others than ever before. This is because you will be giving to them because and if you want
to rather than because you "should" and this kind of help-
because-I-want-to is far more meaningful than merely dutiful giving.

You may have the very high wish to be a channel
through which energy can flow for the good of others. If
so, remember that the energy can flow only if your channel
is open and unblocked. Being on good terms with your inner
being, taking care of it and accepting its guidance, is opening the channel.

We believe that basically what makes human beings
happy is loving, cooperative relationships, giving freely,
and seeing others happy. If really set free, your signal-
giver will lead you toward this. Thus, you do not have to
be afraid it will lead you to selfish, destructive acts. Trust
it and it will be trustworthy.

And finally, your taking care of yourself is good not
only for you, but also for your kid. We have been impressed again and again with how, when people learn to take
better care of themselves, the benefits spill over onto the
other important people in their lives as well. If your kid
is doing things that are on your particular parent's-life
pile, he or she is probably seeing you not as a real, alive
person, but as a kind of shadow, a convenience, a thing.
Your kid may be regarding you in somewhat the same way
he or she would regard a gasoline pump, something to go
to for supplies but which has no feeling, merits no consideration nor even a thank you, and is merely something

to be used. It is not good for a kid to grow up with this view of another person. If you begin taking your own inner signals seriously, your kid, too, will benefit by becoming more aware of you as a real person and learning how to treat people in order to get along in life.

Your kid may be doing everything he or she can to get you to stand up for yourself, because every kid needs a definite, real person to interact with and come up against. By "definite, real person" we mean a person who takes responsibility for getting his or her own needs met, and who does whatever he or she does because he or she wants to. For most kids, the persons who can best be this for them are their parents. Even a therapist cannot give this to a kid the way a parent can.

In short, what has been missing for your kid may well have been the part of you that wants, decides, feels for itself, and takes care of itself. Thus we strongly urge: Put yourself, your wants, needs, and feelings, back into the picture.

Let's begin working on this right now.

The first thing we ask you to do is learn to think and speak in the language of your inner being; that is to say, in *positive I-statements*.

Daring thoughts are constantly welling up inside you just as water wells up from a spring. They originate as I-thoughts.

I want a sandwich.
I itch.
I like that picture.
I feel tired.
I'm going to wash the car.

These are real, decisive, definite communications from you to yourself. They start out ever hopeful that you will hear them and do something about them, but very often they hit a barrier before that can happen. The barrier is made up of a set of fearful ideas like these: If I take care of this original impulse by speaking or acting it out:

> People won't like me.
> It will hurt people's feelings.
> . It will be selfish.
> I will come on too strong.
> It will be impolite.
>> And so on.

The thoughts cannot get through this barrier intact; they can get through only in a weakened, distorted form. They are changed into *questions*, into *you* or *we* or *it statements*, into *negatives*.

Thus, if you are riding along in the country with a friend and the thought, "I want a sandwich," comes up, it's likely to hit the barrier, "To express this thought would be impolite or sound selfish," and to come out as, "When should we stop for a bite?" or "Wouldn't you like to stop for something to eat?" Similarly:

I'm sleepy	can become	Why don't we go to bed?
I feel hurt and unfairly treated	can become	You're no good!
I'm happy	can become	How do you feel?
I want some peace and quiet this summer	can become	Son, why don't you find a job now for summer?

Thus, when the thoughts come out, they're no longer decisive. Notice how each one pushes some kind of responsibility onto whomever it's addressed to. We think that's why they often arouse antagonism in the other person, because actually they foist the decision making upon that person.

Two people who both have this barrier habit of thinking can actually end up doing something neither of them wants.

Would you like to go to the movies?
I don't know. How about you?
I thought maybe you'd like to go.
Well, what would you like to see?
I don't know; what would you like?
I don't think you'd like what's at the Oaks.
Maybe you'd like the one at the Roxian.
    And so on.

We urge you to get back to the original thoughts, the direct, positive I-statements.

We do understand that there are barriers. You may quail at the idea of speaking I-statements, thinking to yourself, "It will hurt other people's feelings," or "People won't like me." These barrier thoughts are strong, and neither of the writers of this book has completely overcome them to this day. Because we've dealt with them for so long, though, we can also tell you some things about them.

These barrier thoughts are very much exaggerated. The fears they inspire are far out of proportion to what is likely actually to happen when you begin to use I-sentences.

The consequences you fear are more likely to come about, not when you use I-sentences, but when you talk in you's!

Within a short time most people experience positive rather than negative effects—improved relationships with others and a sense of exhilaration—after they begin using I's.

When unpleasant results do follow I-sentences, they are usually small and transitory.

The longer term effect of I-sentences on your relationships with others is usually positive.

The next exercise, then, has to do with I-sentences.

Exercise Five

Right now, make some I-thoughts. Complete each of the following sentences in three different ways, and try thinking them, just to see what it feels like:

I feel... (excited, discouraged, hopeful, tired, puzzled, hungry, annoyed, an itch, etc.)

I want... (to go sailing, a better car, to feel happy, to have more friends, etc.)

I'm going to... (try out some of your "wants" here just to see how it feels... or fill in something else, such as: take care of myself, go to bed, read for a while, join the Redwing Club...)

In completing these, let yourself make up some answers without concern over whether they are "true" or not; consider the exercise as play and try out all kinds of sentences, simply to exercise your inner voice.

Take as an assignment that every day for the next week you will make up and speak at least three sentences of the form:

I feel...
I like...
I want...
    or
I am going to...

Leave "you" and "we" out of these sentences until you are completely comfortable using "I".

A note of caution—a sentence with "you" in it can be a you-sentence even if "I feel" or "I want" is part of the sentence. For example, "I feel that you did it on purpose" and "I want you to do it right now" are you-sentences whereas "I feel upset when you use my things" is an I-sentence. Consider a sentence to be a finger. If the finger points back toward you, it is an I-sentence; if it points at someone else, it is a you-sentence.

To speed your learning to think in positive I-statements, simultaneously learn to drop certain other ways of thinking and speaking. There are some verbal expressions that serve to *prevent* you from taking care of yourself. You can learn to substitute other, more honest and effective habits for them.

Exercise Six

Take one of the following speech patterns every day, begin to notice how often you use it, and develop the habit of substituting a different expression for it.

● *Have to*

● *Should*

These expressions imply that *you* are not initiating anything, but are acting only because some outer force decrees you must. Every time you are tempted to use one of these, substitute the words *want to*, and see how this feels for you.

Instead of:	Try:
I have to get to work by three.	I want to get to work by three.
I should make that phone call.	I want to make that phone call.
I have to do that errand.	I want to do that errand.
I should pay those bills.	I want to pay those bills.

● *Negatives* (not, doesn't, can't, won't, isn't, etc.)

A negative tells the listener about something that does not exist, and therefore emphasizes the reverse side of what you actually mean. Whenever you're tempted to use a negative statement, imagine that you've just been stranded on a desert island, and a helicopter pilot, making only one pass overhead, has called out to ask you what you want him to drop you in the way of supplies. It would be best to tell him what you *do* want; if you give him negatives (I *don't* want perfume; I *don't* want evening clothes; I *don't* want enchiladas) you may starve!

In other words, drop the negatives from your language until you can talk comfortably using only positives.

● *Questions*

These, again, simply press your listener to take responsibility for a feeling or idea that originally belonged to you. Change them to positive statements.

Instead of:	Try:
Where were you?	I've been worrying about you, since I was expecting you home at five.
Where would you like to eat?	I'd like to eat at an Italian place tonight.

● *You, we, it*

We understand you could hardly use the language without some of these speech forms. However, to sharpen your idea of how you're actually using them, consider spending a day or two without saying these words except after "if" or "when" and only sparingly even then.

It's paradoxical, but in asking you to work so carefully on your speech patterns, we're actually wanting to help you become more spontaneous, more responsive to your original, inner impulse. In the seventh exercise we ask you directly to become more spontaneous.

Exercise Seven

"Purposely" do some small "spontaneous" things. Resolve to do at least three small, non-duty, fun things every day. Let them come from you, on the spur of the moment.

They need last only two or three minutes if you like.

> Instead of doing dishes right away, first go out and sit on the front steps a few minutes.

> Going out to the car, pick up a pebble and see if you can hit a tree trunk with it.

> In the middle of fixing breakfast, allow a new idea: some raisins might be nice in the orange juice.

If you set yourself to hear them, you may begin to notice all sorts of small, exciting urges from your signal-giver. These are the daring thoughts which in the past you might have squelched.

The above exercises are meant to give you a preliminary sense of what we mean by listening to your own signal-giver. You may have noticed, for example, that you cannot sincerely complete the sentence, "I like..." without first doing a little mental survey of yourself, your situation, what you feel like, to see what you do like. This mental survey is what we mean by consulting yourself; we urge you to get in the habit of consulting yourself regularly and as a matter of course. Every once in a while, throughout your day, take a survey to see what your signals are saying, and allow yourself the thought, "I feel such and so; I'm going to..." and so on.

Now we are coming to perhaps the most difficult idea in this book. It may be hard enough for you to learn to consult your signal-giver when things are going reasonably well in your life. It is important to learn to consult it also *when things go wrong.*

Are you aware of having feelings of worry, dread, anger, and so on now and then during the day? They're likely to come to you in terms of thoughts like this:

> I hate this.
> Ugh.
> Oh, not again!

These experiences are signals from your inner being; it's

trying to say to you, "I'm hurting. Help me!" We think it is very important what you do when such feelings hit you.

You may be into a habit that goes like this:

1. You're going along in your life, and something happens that's negative for you.

>   You realize you have a headache.

>   You remember that you will have to cope with your kid when you get home.

>   You realize you've been cheated somehow.

>   Someone snubs you.

2. You find out that this is negative for you when your signal-giver tells you about it by giving you a painful zing which says, "I'm hurting!"

3. Quick as a flash, you turn your attention away from your signal giver to something in the outside world, and begin struggling with that something. You think (or say):

>   Why is this happening?

>   This is terrible!

>   You are a no-good; you shouldn't do that; stop it!

>   I'm sunk and it's hopeless.

4. Often enough, things get worse.

Thus, although you received a clear message from your signal-giver ("I'm hurting"), you switched your attention away from taking care of it and focussed instead upon something else which you felt was causing your unpleasant feeling—the weather, your kid, the painfulness of your headache, the person who snubbed you. You began using your energy to figure out why that something else behaved so, what that something's behavior means about what you must be, how to stop or get back at or change or placate that something. Notice that all of these thoughts set you up as done-to by something outside yourself. More important, they are *irrelevant* to what you really want. You're hurting, and you want to feel better, and yet not one of these thoughts or remarks will get that for you. Rather, they seem to make the situation even worse.

We think that in switching your attention away from taking care of the hurt your signal-giver described, you deserted that signal-giver. You are like a captain whose ship hits a rock, and who then begins to focus on the rock—figuring out how it got there, whether it is ice or granite, and what this means about his ability as a captain. He'd be a better seaman and have a better chance of surviving if he focussed instead on doing something to take care of his endangered ship. Just so, we think you'd be doing a better job if, when you get a zing, you focus on *taking care of your own being which hurts* instead of shifting your attention to some outside event. Keeping your attention on your own inner being, you could consult it about what would make it feel better and how you might take care of it. It has announced that it is hurting. Act as you might toward a dear friend who told you he or she was hurting, and ask it: "What can I do for you? What will make this hurting better and get you into a better place? What do you really want and how can I go about getting it for you?"

So the new habit can go like this:

1. Something happens that's negative for you.

   Someone snubs you.

2. Your signal-giver tells you about it by giving you a painful zing.

3. You keep your attention focussed on that signal-giver and consult it as to what it wants you to do to make it feel better.

   What do I want to do right now?

4. Then you wait a moment, keeping your attention focussed not on the disturbing event (the person who
snubbed you) but on whatever inside you tells you
what you like and don't like. If you're in pretty good
touch with it, ideas about what things to do will begin to come to you. They may or may not have to
do with the thing that disturbed you.

Actually, I'm hot and I want to go take a shower.

I want a good relationship with this person who
snubbed me, and I'm curious as to why he's upset. I'll tell him that.

I want to be away from this person. Therefore
I'll leave the room.

I feel hurt and a dinner out will make me feel
taken care of. Therefore I'm going.

The great advantage of waiting to act until you get
the message from your inner being is that now, whatever
you do, you will be doing it because you choose to and
want to, rather than because you are acted upon automatically, like a robot.

The first few times you do this, you may receive and
act upon answers that result in more discomfort for you
in some way, rather than making you feel better. If this
happens, you know that you have not listened well enough
to your inner signal-giver. It knows what you most deeply
want, and it will give you signals of discomfort about any
answer that is wrong for you. You need only become more
aware of it and commit yourself more deeply to being loyal
to it.

Your son calls you a bad name. You consult your signal-
giver about what would make you feel better, and the first
answer you get is, "Hit him," or "Slap him!" You hit your
son—and then you feel worse rather than better; you've
won the current battle but you feel guilty and discouraged
about the total situation. Now, looking back at the answer,

"Hit him," you realize that a nagging feeling of "not quite right" accompanied it; you were not completely relaxed and sure about it.

Here the job would be to wait for further answers. Feel OK about doing nothing at all about the situation until you get a clear message from yourself. Hearten yourself, and wait for an answer that feels good when you are in a heartened mood.

What if no answers come? Sometimes parents are quite out of the practice of hearing their inner voices, and say to us, "I don't *know* what I want to do." "No answer comes!" If this happens, we suggest that you *prime* your signal-giver so that it can begin giving you answers. Purposely think of all the possible ways you might behave, and present them all to your inner being, letting it approve or disapprove each choice. Think of dozens of choices for it.

How about telling this person off?

How about ignoring him or her?

How about getting yourself a drink?

Do you want to go roller skating?

How about going over and giving this person a hug?

How about fighting back?

How about calling a friend and talking about skiing?

How about calling the police?

How about leaving right now and spending the night in a motel?

How about going to do my favorite activity?

And so on.

Your signal giver will deliver a precise degree of approval or disapproval for each choice, and you can then take the one with the highest approval.

Our overall point is this: that you may have been letting your inner being down in the bad times by ignoring it, failing to take care of it, and finally doing things that get you results you do not really want. We urge you to redirect your loyalty. Promise yourself that *every time you feel a zing you will keep your head and do your best to get for your inner being what it most truly wants.*

Some of the unpleasant events you experience are things over which you have little influence, such as the weather. Others you can change, or at least reduce the chance of their happening in the future. For these we will describe, in subsequent chapters, some specific ways of acting which can be instrumental in getting you what you want when these negative things happen to you. However, whether you can change the distressing outside event or not, taking care of your own inner voice, as we have been urging in this chapter, is vital.

The most important single thing you can do for yourself and for your kid is to take hold of your own life and make it what you want and do what you truly want with it. Commit yourself to be loyal to and take care of your inner being.

Six

Preparing to Stand Up

We're beginning work now on the items on the rest of your list—the troubling things your kid does which do have an effect on your life. We will assume that you have gone carefully through the earlier part of this book and have already backed off from trying to control your kid's life in areas that affect only him or her, if you ever were— so that what's left are items like the following which do seem to have an effect on your life.

Won't do chores.
Uses foul language around the house; calls me names.
Leaves messes in the house.
Uses my clothes, hairdryer, transistor radio, without asking; gives them to friends.
Steals my money, liquor, jewelry.
Doesn't clean up her dog's messes.
Racks up long distance phone bills.
Grows pot in the house; stores it in his room.
Knocks holes in the walls when he gets angry.
Uses my tools and leaves them out in the rain.
Wrecked my car.
Demands money.

Has friends, parties, in the house while we are at work.

Freeloads; will neither go to school nor work.

Is hurting my relationship with my partner.

Some of these are things that lead a counselor to say to the parent, in real wonderment, "Why in the world do you put up with it?" and sometimes to go further and recommend, "Don't put up with it!" However, the parent usually *doesn't know how* to stop putting up with it. This is what we want to show you.

We think that these parent's-life items get to you not because of what they are in themselves. You'd probably gladly do the work, undergo the pain, provide the things, clean up the messes, if doing these things were part of effective kid raising and you got the satisfaction of doing a good job and having a good relationship out of it. We think they get to you because of what they mean. When your kid does these things, it's as though he or she were saying:

I don't care about you.

You're not a valuable person.

I don't have to pay attention to you.

You don't matter.

They hurt, then, because of the way they define you and your kid. They say that he or she is irresponsible and inconsiderate, and that you are merely a convenience or a shadow whose rights need not be considered.

If things like the above items are happening to you, we believe there's a sense in which you have allowed yourself to be taken too much as a convenience. You are being too much a doormat, a pushover.

Being a doormat is largely a matter of *your* attitude.

To get you out of this trouble with your kid, we propose to teach you to stand up and leave the doormat attitude behind forever.

There are two general things to learn in order to

do this. One is some specific techniques of assertiveness, which we will coach you on in Chapters 7 through 9. The other is an attitude—an attitude of feeling comfortable, relaxed, loving toward your kid because you know you will take care of yourself and therefore your happiness is not at risk in the situation. In this chapter we will review ways of acting or thinking which we think contribute to such an attitude. You may or may not want to accept all of these ideas as right for you, but we do ask that you study them enough so that you understand them. We think the attitude they reflect is basic to your success in resolving the problems with your kid and in becoming as happy as you'd like in your own life.

We've touched on all of these ideas in earlier parts of this book, so they won't be entirely new to you. Consider them now, one by one, as a checkup to put yourself into an appropriate frame of mine before tackling the assertive assignments of the next three chapters.

Hold Your Goals in Mind

When you're feeling pressed about something that's happening between you and your kid, remember what your basic goal is. You want:

To be happier yourself.

To see your kid be a responsible and decent person.

Hold onto this idea so that you do not let yourself be hooked into the irrelevant emotions we talked about in Chapter 6.

What most people most deeply want is happiness and fair, cooperative relationships with others. We believe that both you and your kid do too. However, under stress or threat, people tend to forget all about what they are truly after and begin to operate as if their deepest concerns were:

Who's going to win.

Proving I'm right.

Showing I can control my kid.

Proving that I am a good parent.

What other people will think.

What the society says things should be like.

and even

What the law says I must do.

We've not heard a parent say that what he or she most deeply wanted was one of these things, but we've seen a lot of parents act as if it were. That's very human behavior, but in the long run it perpetuates the very problem the parent is struggling to change. We ask you to keep your head in the sense of keeping your perspective and remembering what you are really after even through stressful times and setbacks.

In moments of stress, stay with your heartening, and remember that what you're after is a happier situation for yourself and a responsible and decent kid.

Hold a Positive View of Your Kid

Look at your kid's misbehavior in a different way. You may have been believing that your kid does troublesome things simply because he or she wants to, or is basically lazy, dishonest, careless, immature, or dislikes you. In Chapter 3 we asked you to begin looking at them in a different way. Look at them as things your kid does in order to keep him or herself defined as lazy, dishonest, and so forth, because he or she is afraid of standing up as a solid, responsible, good person, and these things enable him or her to play the irresponsible role. Consider them as precisely designed to get you to reinforce this definition by getting helplessly angry, feeling hurt, trying to force the kid to stop it, seeing him or her as a bad person and yourself as a bad, helpless parent. We ask that rather than continuing to function in this role for your kid, you do something different.

Believe that your kid already is basically a solid, responsible, good person, and that he or she, like everyone else, basically wants a fair, loving, cooperative relationship with the people in his or her life. When you confront the kid, speak to the basic part of him or her that wants this.

Your Attitude—It Can Actually Change Things

The way you *see* the situation between you and your kid *influences* it. The attitude you take not only helps you decide how to act, but even more striking, your attitude influences your kid's attitude and actions.

Attitudes are highly contagious. The attitude you're in when you relate with another person will powerfully influence the other to see things within the same general framework. Try it—look straight into the eyes of the next person you meet and give either a warm smile or a scowl, and notice its immediate impact on the other.

This influence is especially important in the parent-kid relationship, simply because you are the parent, and the kid is geared to expect authority and expertise from elders, despite what he or she may say or imply to the contrary. Thus your attitude can influence your kid more than his or her attitude influences yours. Take responsibility for setting the mood and the atmosphere between you and your kid, then, and don't let yourself get pulled into a contest, a who's-going-to-win attitude, even if that's where your kid is.

Recognize that simply holding a positive attitude about your kid will influence the problem you're having with him or her in a positive way.

An Equal Relationship

Consider what a relationship of equality between you and your kid would be like. If you're having trouble, a basic problem is likely to be that your relationship with your son or daughter has shifted from one of equality to one in which one (or both) of you is trying to control the other—towards, in other words, a master-slave relationship. In the first half of this book we asked you to reverse any tendency toward your being the master, the kid the slave. It will be equally important now to reverse any tendency toward your being the slave, the kid the master.

You can reverse a you-slave, kid-master tendency by taking your wants and rights as seriously as you do anyone else's, including your kid's, and standing up for them with all the passion that you would for any exploited being.

You began working on this in Chapter 5 and should go farther with it now.

Examine your own ideas about the relationship, and see whether any of the following are among them:

I'm obliged to support and care for my kid. He or she is under no obligation to me.

I'm responsible for him or her. He or she is not responsible for me.

My kid has a right to be supported and cared for by me without making any return. I have no particular rights in the situation.

We've heard many parents and kids express variations of this one-way view. Parents say things like:

I'm obligated. I owe it to her to take care of her.

I have to put up with it; he's my kid.

I'll start living my own life when they get out on their own.

Kids say things which mirror the same ideas, ideas that their parents are obliged to put up with them and to take anything that they do until they reach a certain age. A conversation one of us had with a fifteen-year old boy recently exemplifies this view.

"Who does the cooking around here?"

"Mom."

"What about cleaning the place up?"

"Mom."

"Trash?"

"Mom puts it in the garage and Dad puts it out on Wednesdays when he goes to work."

"How about the yard?"

"Dad likes to mess around out there on weekends."

"Who changes the sheets and makes the beds?"

"Mom."

"All of them?"

"Yeah."

"How come?"

(Shrug) "That's her job."

"What's yours?"

(Shrug) "I guess nothing. But Mom doesn't work so taking care of us is her job."

Here are three further actual examples we have observed.

Karl (13) had just made a shambles of his father's workshop and another mess in the kitchen fixing himself a snack. His father asked him to clean things up, but Karl simply got on his motorbike for his usual late night at the pinball parlor. When his father said, "Well, I'm not going to let you in until things are cleaned up," Karl laughed and said, "You have to; you're obligated."

Ann (14) had friends in the house for pot parties during school hours, while her mother was at work. She stayed out as late as she pleased at night, failed to clean up after herself in the house, and refused to do chores. Asked why her mother put up with all this and continued to support her, she said simply, "She has to."

Jeff (17) had just wrecked his mother's car and left it some miles away on the highway. He had not done any chores nor contributed to the family for many months. When his mother expressed her utter frustration, he leaned back in his easy chair and said in mock comfort, "Well, only one more year, baby!"

Kids with this view of their parents tend not to feel grateful for what those parents do for them; rather, they may be resentful because their "servants" are not doing more. We've talked with kids who honestly felt cheated because their parents didn't provide them with cars, or because the ones they were given were not good enough. Obviously, these kids feel that it is their right to be supported and taken care of, given to, without making any return. Then they feel abused and angry when their parents' offerings do not meet their expectations.

If any of this fits the way things have been going between you and your kid, then we think it's time for you to make a Declaration of Human Rights for yourself, and resolve to uphold it. Consider substituting for the above attitudes, ideas like:

My kid and I have equal rights as human beings.

My kid is responsible to take care of his or her own wants and happiness, and I am responsible for mine.

My first task is to be loyal to my own inner being; doing that will actually be helpful to those around me.

The best parent is neither a slave nor a master, but an equal human being.

The best thing I can give my kids is a model that it is OK to take care of one's own feelings, wants, and ideas, and to be happy.

In summary of this idea of equality, then, consider moving toward a relationship of equality between you and your kid.

Your Rights

If you have decided you do want a more equal relationship with your son or daughter, decide now what your rights are, and commit yourself to stand up for them.

How can you tell what your rights are?

At first thought, it may seem to you that your rights are something you inherently have, as much a part of you and as unchangeable as your ears and hands. However, when you realize that people have very different "rights" in different times and different parts of the world, you begin to see that there is no such thing as an inherent right.

Your "rights" are what you and the people in your life believe or agree they are. For example, if you and the government believe or agree that you have the right to own property, then you do. If there is no such belief or agreement, then you don't. *And if you are not satisfied with the rights you have in any current situation, it's up to you to pick out and claim new rights for yourself that you think would be more fair.* It's always been this way with rights between people. For example, in olden days the "right to vote" simply did not exist; there was no such thing. Then people invented this right, claimed it and struggled for it, and from then on the "right to vote" did exist. At first, though, men had this right and women didn't, and during the time covered by this decision, that was "right"— because people in general agreed that it was. Then women claimed this right and struggled to establish it for themselves, and now it's generally agreed that they do have it.

In other words, your rights do not exist anywhere in any absolute sense; it's up to you to make them up and claim them.

When you do decide you want some rights you have not been accorded lately, prepare yourself to stand up for them. (We will show you how in the next chapters). This standing up is necessary because if other people have been catered to for some time they tend to think they should be catered to, that this is their right, and they will object when you suggest something different. If your kid has been walking on you for some time, he or she may well assume this is the way things *should* be, and will defend it. In a sense, by not claiming your right to equality, you have let your son or daughter believe you don't have that right, and now he or she is used to this. Therefore, when you first claim new rights, you will probably have to retrain your kid to accept them. It's as though a gardener's son and a prince had been playing checkers over the years, and the gardener's son has always held back so that the prince could win. After some time both are likely to assume that the prince has the right to win and the gardener's son doesn't—simply because it's always been that way. If the gardener's son now wants to re-establish his "right" to a fair win, he'll have some re-training to do, and the prince may very well object, feel unfairly treated and resentful.

We've noticed that kids act very much like princes when previously humble parents begin to stand up. Consider the following true story of a sixteen year old boy who actually threatened to run away because his father would not buy him a (third) new car.

> A well-to-do father provided cars for all of his children when they reached sixteen. The fourth kid wrecked his new car, so the father provided another. When this one was also wrecked, the father declined to provide a third. The kid now felt genuinely resentful and unfairly treated! He had become used to the idea that Dad provides cars, and he felt Dad had no *right* to withhold one.

Now, we think that if your kid has been doing the kinds of things we're talking about in this chapter, it's very likely that you have been accorded fewer rights than you'd like and than you think is fair. We'd like to see you decide upon some new, more fair rights for yourself and then commit yourself utterly to taking care of them. Be ready to work to establish a new view of the fairness of your rights in your kid, as the voters, the gardener's son, and the father had to do in the above examples. You will have to provide a new definition of your rights, and stand up for them.

Here are some sample rights other parents have decided they want and will stand up for.

- The right to privacy.
- The right to my own relationships with my spouse and friends.
- The right to be free of fear of violence.
- The right to feel secure about my belongings.
- The right to some time of my own.
- The right to be treated with courtesy.
- The right to relationships that are two-way rather than only one-way streets.
- The right to reasonable peace and quiet.
- The right to feel everyone is carrying his or her weight and I am not supporting a freeloader.
- The right to close up my house in the evening and know no one will come in after that.

By the way, these "rights" are not so very different from the things kids say they want for themselves. Be sure you're granting your kid rights equivalent to those you now want for yourself, so that you can have a truly equal relationship! It will not work to claim any of these basic rights for yourself while withholding it from your kid.

How does the law fit in with this question of your rights? Many parents (and we did the same ourselves) think it is useless to consider what their rights are because they're "legally responsible" for their kids. They take this to mean that they're legally bound to support their kids, make them behave properly, put up with whatever they do, without recourse, and pay for any damages they incur. Naturally, this makes them feel hopeless about claiming any rights for themselves.

The good news here is that, although indeed the law

in your state probably does state that you are responsible for your kid, it's much more reasonable than most parents realize, and it need not at all prevent you from claiming basic human rights in the relationship with your kid.

We know of no law anywhere that says you must put up with the kind of behavior we're talking about in this chapter. In most states the law regarding parents and kids is two-way. As as example of representative legislation on this subject, California law (and it is civil rather than criminal law) requires the parent or guardian to support and to provide a home and care for a minor child. *The same body of law requires that the minor attend school and obey the reasonable and proper orders or directions of his or her parent or guardian and of school authorities.*

It's true that you can be assessed for damages your kid might incur—but, in the first place, there is likely to be a legal limit to your financial responsibility. In California, for example, that limit is $5,000 for each instance of injury or damage, which means that although you'd be very hurt financially, you would probably not be completely ruined. In the second place, there's no point in letting your behavior be determined by fear of this eventuality, because you can't control it whether you claim your rights or not. Letting yourself be walked on by your kid doesn't save you from the possibility of being sued, so you might as well claim your rights. Actually, we think that kids are less likely to act out and do damage when parents stand up for themselves.

In summary of this discussion of your rights, *decide right now what your rights are and commit yourself to stand up for them.*

Fear of Encounter

The next thing to do, after you've decided what your fair rights are and that you will stand up for them, is to begin coming to terms with your fears of the encounters you may have to undergo when you claim those rights.

Parents sometimes put up with a lot from their kids because they dread the disapproving or disappointed or an-

gry looks or the scene that might result if they stood up
for themselves. This is quite natural. Nobody enjoys dis-
harmony and the really terrible position of standing out all
alone against opposition. One of us very well remembers
the experience of this fear, over and over again, in situations like this:

> I had told our kids I wanted no snacking out of the refrig-
> erator in the hour before dinnertime. I was sitting in the
> living room at about 5:30 when I heard our son, 16, come
> into the kitchen and open the refrigerator. I knew the next
> step I wanted to take was to give him an I-sentence re-
> minder: "Son, I really want no snacking before dinnertime."
> I was so afraid to say it that I began literally to shake.
> The temptation was almost overwhelming to *pretend that I
> had not heard him and therefore would not have to say it.*

This fear of encounter is of course justified in one
sense. It's true that you may indeed get some sour looks
or scenes as you begin to stand up for yourself, especially
if you've been walked on for some time. Even though he
or she very much needs the limits you will set, no kid of
any spirit is going simply to accept them and say, "Thanks."
It's part of the game to fight back for what the kid thinks
are his or her rights. And kids can do all sorts of things
to pressure you into backing down once you've begun to
stand up. They can say things like:

> You don't care about me.
> I hate you.
> I'll run away.
> I wish I (or you) were dead.

They can give you the silent treatment, or the gloomy,
I'm-so-mistreated treatment. They can have tantrums and
break things.

> Linda (15) had been hanging back from doing any chores
> for some time. Her mother asked her to sweep the floor.
> Saying nothing, Linda walked out the door and left home
> as a runaway.

Arlene (16) was in the habit of pestering her mother for the car every morning. Her mother would stall, make excuses, and finally give in to her. One day her mother said "No," whereupon Arlene swept all the dishes off the breakfast table. When her mother stood firm in the no, Arlene seriously threatened to push her ailing grandmother into the swimming pool.

Carol (14) used to come home well after suppertime and then snack on leftovers in the kitchen, but she never cleaned up after herself. Her mother requested that she do so and stuck to the request, upon which Carol threw a tantrum in which she broke many of the things in her room and screamed so loudly that the neighbors became alarmed and called the police.

Now, we know that the prospect of any of these behaviors can be frightening. We also believe that the less afraid of them you are, the less likely they are to happen. That's because these are blackmailing behaviors—things the kid does to pressure you into giving in to him or her. No kid is going to waste tantrums on someone who clearly is not impressed by them.

Further, there's a sense in which the fear of encounter is not justified. It's this. We think that what you're most deeply afraid of here is not what the kid will do. You could probably stand most of that very well if it weren't directed at you. What you actually most dread may be the idea of yourself standing out in everyone's view as a real, solid person who dares to hold up his or her head and say, "I claim these rights for myself." We well know that this can indeed be a scary thing. We also know that, far from being actually harmful or dangerous, standing out in this direct way is the very essence of good human communication.

If you've been dreading the encounters, it may well be because you feel helpless about them, do not know what to do during them. Having something definite to do will ease this fear. We'll be giving you that in the chapters that follow. So let yourself realize that you will have all the tools you need to handle encounters.

Realize, too, that in the encounter you are actually giving your kid the most precious thing you can—a piece of yourself—and he or she very much needs some of yourself from you.

Also, if you're afraid of encounters in general, realize that this situation with your kid is a chance for you to free yourself of that fear. You can learn to be comfortable with the scenes and even enjoy them—come to look forward to the feeling of exhilaration and accomplishment you get from knowing you can handle them.

An exercise: If you can, listen to some younger kids talking together—kids between say five and ten. Notice how outspoken they are—flagrant, forthright, bossy. They seem unafraid of encounter. As an adult, you have so much more life experience than these little ones; what would it be like if your riches came tumbling out in this way? You and everyone else would know you're alive and maybe all of you would thrill to the encounter!

Thus, regarding encounters, you will have the tools to handle them and they can be exhilarating. After you have successfully dealt with a few of them, you will feel more at ease with them and also will probably notice that they become less frequent and less intense.

Being Open

In Chapter 5 we asked you to begin becoming more sensitive to what your own wants, discomforts, feelings are, and to drop out I-sentences telling about them. When you do this you are doing a number of things. You are being open; you are taking a first step in the direction of taking care of yourself; and you are giving something of yourself to the other person in direct communication. *You are also developing a habit that can be counted on to carry you through every interaction.* Whenever an uncomfortable feeling comes over you—fear of the encounter, worry about the outcome, confusion over what to do or say next, or any uncomfortable feeling, you can begin to take care of yourself by focussing on your inner being, asking what it is experiencing, and then expressing that experience to whomever confronts you:

> I'm stuck about what to say. I just don't know what to say.

> I feel absolutely helpless about this.

> I'm so worried the house will burn down.

With every bit of genuine openness like this, spoken as I-sentences and without you's, you will find your power coming back to you and the situation progressing toward greater equality.

Realize that a major aspect of bringing about an equal relationship and resolving these parent's-life items is your own openness.

In summary, the attitude we are encouraging you to develop, as you work on the parent's-life items, involves these aspects:

Stay with your heartening, and remember that what you're after is your own happiness and a responsible kid who can make his or her own decisions.

Assume that your kid is basically a solid, responsible person who is doing these troublesome things because he or she has little practice in standing out as a good and competent person and is afraid to do so.

Understand that by taking this attitude toward the situation you are already beginning to improve it.

Take as your goal an equal-human-beings relationship between you and your kid.

Decide upon your fair rights in the relationship and resolve to stand up for them. Realize that if you can count on yourself to take care of your own rights, you can be relaxed and confident no matter how any specific interaction turns out.

Realize there may be some encounters, and expect that your hesitancy about them can change to confidence and even pleasant anticipation as you practice handling them.

Count on your own openness as a major tool in all of this.

Seven

Eliminating Triggers

and Reinforcers

Now we are ready to begin working on the specific problems that may be left after you have sincerely worked through the first six chapters of this book.

Please review and revise your list of parent's-life items at this point. That list may have shifted and changed and some items may even have disappeared when you handed responsibility for the kid's-life items over to your son or daughter. Prune the list down to things that are still problems for you, including things that have come up within the last week or two after you dropped efforts to control kid's-life items. Your revised list may include any of the parent's-life items listed on pages 2 and 85-86, and any aspects reserved from kid's-life items in Chapter 2.

Now let's begin working on that up-dated list.

As a first step, look for any obvious ways in which, unknowingly, you may actually have been *inviting* the behavior on this list. Bear each item in mind as you read this chapter and consider carefully anything you may have been doing to make it more likely to happen.

Parents help bring about the very behavior that bothers them in two ways: by *triggering* it before it starts, and by *reinforcing* it after it's been done. The trigger is usually

Issues

Date Due	Title	Barcode
04/09/2009	How to deal with your acting-up teenager :	33550001008742
04/09/2009	The comprehensive preschool curriculum /	33550009458634
04/09/2009	The early childhood years :	33550006277383

some form of you-message or a question. The reinforcement is negative attention. That's why we encourage you, when you're coping with these misbehaviors, to *make I-statements* instead of you-messages or questions, and to focus *positive, helping attention* on *yourself* instead of negative attention on your kid.

Let's go over some of the specific ways in which you may be triggering or reinforcing the very behavior that is so bothersome to you. We'll talk about five kinds of items that are especially likely to be encouraged by parents.

> Lying.
> Stealing.
> Saying worrisome or frightening things, name-calling, swearing.
> Having a sullen or belligerent attitude.
> Abusing favors a parent has granted.

● Lying.

If your kid's lying has been one of your problems, you may be getting less of it now that you have handed him or her responsibility for the kid's-life items. That's because kids sometimes lie when they must ask your permission for kid's-life items and think you may say No. If Marilyn, for instance, wants to go to the shopping mall with a friend who has recently been picked up for shoplifting, it's tempting for her to say to you in a lie: "Mom, may I go to Paula's tonight? We're going to work on our school project." According to the old way of doing things, you'd be likely to give your permission to this, and she could then go to the mall feeling righteously that she has successfully fooled the dictator. However, if you've given up the job of permitting or forbidding activities, as we asked you to in Chapters 2 through 4, your kid cannot so easily justify lying, and is less likely to do it. According to the new way, if Marilyn still asks your permission for an innocent night at her friend's house, you will say only, "I'm glad you told me; I'll know to hold supper then," or perhaps, "I'm out of the permission-giving business, but thanks for letting me know where you'll be." You haven't picked up her lie; you've left her stuck with it. Marilyn will then have to go to the mall knowing that she has unnecessarily lied to you; there's no dictator to justify her lying for her. This is less comfortable for her than the old way, and there's more room for her to be straight with you instead and to say, "Mom, I'm going to the mall with Susan tonight"—without lies. There's more room for you, too, since you've given up forbidding her or granting permission, to express concern, interest, and trust. "I'm uncomfortable with that because I worry that Susan might shoplift again and perhaps get you both into trouble. And yet I know you'll do what's right for you about going."

Even if you've given your son or daughter responsibility for the kid's-life items, though, you may still be getting other lies, about all sorts of things. If so, look to see whether you are *triggering lies by asking questions*, and *reinforcing them by focussing negative attention on your kid when he or she lies*.

Begin with the resolve to ask your kid no questions whatsoever for at least a week.

This probably won't be as difficult as it sounds. Simply stay a little alert to the way you talk with your son or daughter, and every time you feel the impulse to ask a question, either say nothing at all, or change the question to something you can express as an I-statement.

Instead of:	Try this:
Have you done your chores yet?	I'd like to know the bathroom is clean by now.
Why don't you say hello to me when I come home?	I feel left out when I don't get a hello.
	or
	I'd like a hello when I get home at night.
How are you getting home?	I worry about your safety and I'd like to know you'll be getting home safely.

Is your homework done?	Say Nothing! (A clear kid's-life item).

There's one kind of question we especially caution against—the question in which you test whether your kid will lie by asking about something you already know. For example:

> The school called home to ask whether Jennifer (14) was ill, since she had not come to school. That afternoon Jennifer's mother asked her, "How was school today?"

We think this is entrapment. We recommend against it partly because it is likely to induce a lie from Jennifer and thus give her more practice at the very thing her mother doesn't want, and even more because asking this sort of question has the same elements of deceit and manipulation as the lying itself. A simple statement and an I-message would be more effective:

> The principal called today to ask why you weren't at school. I hate to get calls from the school and would really appreciate freedom from that sort of call.

When you stop the questions, the lies are likely to decline dramatically. You may still get a few that your kid volunteers because he or she doesn't yet realize you're out of the lying hassle; for these, be sure that when you hear them, you do something different from giving your kid negative attention. Any kind of worried or angry reaction will feed the lying habit, so instead do something like this:

> Simply say "Hm" and walk away to do your favorite thing.

> Pretend you're listening to a neighbor kid telling you something in a friendly discussion in which, even if you privately think he or she is lying, there's no need to check it out, and you can be simply polite.

Say, "I'm uncomfortable because I keep getting the feeling I'm being lied to, so I'd like to stop this conversation."

If you make sure you've truly stopped questions and negative attention, we can't promise you'll get as good results as Kathy's mother did in the following true life experience. Yet we wouldn't be surprised either. The strategy is so often successful that we've come to feel that lying is one of the easiest problems for parents to deal with.

Mrs. R. complained that Kathy (8) lied almost continuously. She lied about her own activities ("I got an A in school today") and she also "made up" tall tales about things she had seen and heard. Investigation showed that Mrs. R. asked questions almost continuously, all the way from, "How are you?" and "How was school?" to "What are you doing now?" "Why did you steal my cosmetics?" "What are you going to do next?" and "Don't you want to be good?" and "Why do you lie?" She was coached to stop all questions, and instead either make I-statements or keep silence. In other words, she was to stop triggering Kathy's lies. She was also told to respond to any colorful tales with a genuine expression of interest, if she felt it: "That's interesting!" In other words, she was to stop reinforcing Kathy's lies by giving them negative attention. She made a heroic turn-about, following our suggestions to the letter. Though we all expected a longer-term struggle with the lies, they stopped immediately.

Of course, when the lying stops you may also realize that what bothered you was not just the lying itself, but the thing the lying was *about*. If your kid is lying about going to school, or about marijuana, or about whether he or she has stolen your jewelry, it won't solve your problem if only the lying stops. You want the truancy, drug abuse, or stealing to stop. In such a case, congratulate yourself on being able to stop the lying! Then deal with the other, underlying, problem directly. If it's a kid's-life item, re-read Chapters 2-4. If it's a parent's-life problem continue through this chapter and the next ones.

● Stealing.

Sometimes parents report things like this:

I get paid in cash, and my son Tom (16) seeks it out wherever I put it and steals some of it.

Sandra (14) takes my clothes and jewelry and sells them to her friends.

Ralph (16) brought two friends in the house while I was on a business trip and let them go through my closet. They found $65 grocery money I'd left for my wife, and they took it.

Parents often begin a two-step program of reinforcing-and-triggering stealing right after the first theft occurs. They do it by (1) focussing negative attention on the person who stole, by scolding, asking questions, punishing—and by (2) proceeding to leave valuable things available to be taken the next time. The more the stealing worries them and the more they want to be able to trust their kids, the more likely they are to do these things.

The basic thing they can do to resolve the stealing problem is anything different from these two behaviors. Your job is to decide upon definite ways to act that will not give your kid negative attention and will not invite him or her to steal again. There's room for all sorts of creative decisions about what to do instead, and any of them is likely to work even better if you pick it out yourself. That's because *what* you do is less important than that it be something you can do while feeling comfortable and relaxed, without emotional charge, and you know best what that would be. For example, you might use each theft as a signal to you to begin your favorite activity, announcing to all (including the probable thief) that you were doing so in order to ease the pain of the theft. Another possibility would be to give the stolen object to the thief.

In a story by Victor Hugo, a man stole some silver plates from a priest who had given him food and shelter. When, later, gendarmes brought him to the priest to check out his claim that the treasures they found in his possession had been given to him, the priest announced that indeed they were a gift. This giving of the precious silver was a crucial turning point in the man's life, leading him to a much better way of living.

Again, the crucial feature of each solution is not the behavior itself, but rather that you feel relaxed and unworried as you do it. If solutions like these above leave you feeling that you are not being taken care of, consider the following two straightforward and practical steps.

First, make sure you're not inviting the stealing by leaving stealable things around when you know there's a stealing problem in your house. Look at the kind of thing that's getting stolen; If you'd lock it up in a strange hotel room, do the same in your house. You won't leave purses or wallets, loose cash or jewelry, or even appealing little things like electronic watches and transistor radios lying about if you sincerely mean to keep them and you know stealing has been going on.

Tell your kid in an I-message that you're going to make your things secure. For instance, "Carol, I've noticed that some of my cash has disappeared, so I'm going to keep it elsewhere from now on."

Many are the parents we have coached to do this.

Mary's mother was raising two kids alone in cramped quarters; the only private place she allowed herself was a box on top of the closet shelf, where she kept jewelry, cigarettes, and some change. Several times a week she would notice some of these things were missing, and she and Mary (13) would then have a fight about it. The pattern of the fights was quite constant: Mother would ask whether Mary had taken something, Mary would deny, Mother accuse, Mary would get angry, Mother would cry. We coached Mary's mother to stop all questions, accusations, and crying, and obtain a sturdy lock for her box.

There was a continual shadow over Roger (15) in his family. Father had a jar full of old pennies in the closet, and every time the level seemed a little lower than it had been, both parents suspected Roger had taken some. He, of course, denied it. We recommended to the father that he lock up the pennies.

Making your things secure will probably not be enough to resolve the stealing problem for you. For one thing, if that's all you do, your kid may take it as a game or a contest, and manage to seek out the hiding places, break the locks, pry open the drawers. For another, you probably don't want to lock things up in your own house until your kid is old enough to leave home.

The second, more difficult, thing we ask you to do is to turn off any negative attention and substitute a cheerful taking care of yourself when you think you've been stolen from.

We have no doubt that kids steal because they are afraid to stand up and be defined as good, happy, responsible people, and stealing is an easy way to keep themselves safely defined as bad and irresponsible. Kids could acquire almost anything they steal in other ways, but those other ways would involve being upfront and perhaps industrious and would define them as being responsible. Stealing, on the other hand, proves they are no-good—and that's why they do it. The best way of combating the stealing, then, is to make sure it does not work for the kid—that is, that it does not brand him or her as bad, through negative attention—and to do what you can to enable him or her to become comfortable with feeling like a good and responsible person. *Telling* your kid he or she is good won't do this, but you can do it by being a model for your kid, showing him or her that you yourself feel good, happy, and responsible, that you will take care of yourself, and that you cannot be provoked into giving negative attention. With you as a model, the kid can then little by little take courage to feel good and responsible, and will no longer need the stealing to prove otherwise.

How do you cheerfully take care of yourself when your kid has stolen from you? We ask you to do just the sort of thing you'd do if a piece of the roof fell in—that is, act to get it fixed, perhaps ask for help, and in any case, give not any scolding nor blaming to your kid at all. You are the one who's been injured by being robbed, and your job now is to do something to make it up to yourself. Here are a few examples to show how taking care of yourself might go. Notice that all avoid negative attention upon the kid and emphasize, instead, I-messages and a focus on getting fair treatment for yourself.

Suppose that you notice that money is missing from your purse or wallet. Of your two kids, Bill has taken money before and you therefore suspect that he has done it this time too, although you are not sure. You say,

"Mabel and Bill, I've just noticed that there is $10 missing from my purse. I'd like help in getting it back."

"I didn't take it."

"Me neither."

"I understand what you're saying, and I'm saying I want it back. If I don't get it back by tomorrow, we may be eating a lot of bean soup next week, since that was part of the grocery money."

The next step may be that you or someone else "finds" the money. It mysteriously turns out to be in your purse after all, or Bill unexpectedly "finds" it in the kitchen drawer where you usually keep your purse (we have had instances in which just this has happened). If the money shows up like this, accept it casually, and resist sarcasm. If it does not, then serve a great deal of bean soup until you've recovered the equivalent of your $10 for yourself.

With variations to fit the individual situation, we've coached many parents whose kids have been stealing from them to take care of themselves.

Ralph (16) was a quiet, rather shy boy who very much wanted friends. One day his father came home from a business trip and found that $65 was missing from his closet. Ralph gave him the following explanation. He had been very impressed by two older boys he met who talked rough and were obviously more sophisticated in the ways of the world than he While his parents were out, he had invited these boys into the house and did not object when they went through his parents' bedroom. They found $65 in Ralph's father's closet, and promptly disappeared with it. Upon hearing this, Ralph's dad called the police; however, there turned out to be confusion about who and where the two boys were and exactly who had the money now. We coached the father to treat the matter just as he would if an equal-age friend had lost some of his (Dad's) money. There was neither scolding nor punishment of Ralph; Dad simply told him that he considered Ralph responsible for the house and everything in it while the parents were away, and that he expected the money to be replaced. Ralph agreed to pay it from his after-school job. Dad also told Ralph he wanted no strangers in the house when he wasn't there, and that if he had to, to feel comfortable while away, he would hire a house-sitter, though he would much rather count on Ralph to take care of him in this matter.

Tricia (15) and Marilyn (16) were two volatile and dramatic sisters who felt free to do whatever occurred to them to further their fun. They regularly made themselves free with their mother's possessions and seemed unmoved by her complaints, accusations, pleas, and even crying about it. One day she was especially disconcerted to see that an expensive sweater had disappeared from her closet. This time she simply told her daughters firmly, "I want my sweater back." The girls of course denied knowledge of the sweater; they shouted, became sullen, claimed unfair treatment. At one point one of them stormed furiously out of the house rather than answer her mother. Mother was able to stay fairly relaxed and comfortable through all this because she knew exactly what she would do no matter what the girls did, and because she focussed on what she was going to do rather than on her daughters. She simply stood firm and repeatedly made only one response to anything the girls said or did: "I want my sweater back." After several hours of this, she also told the girls, "I want my sweater back, and if I don't get it by tonight I will definitely ransack your closets and throw your clothes in the swimming pool."* She was obviously prepared to do just this. Even-

---

* More later on taking physical actions like this. They can rebound unless they're thought out ahead of time and you are utterly sincere and committed about them.

tually Marilyn broke down and, weeping, said, "Well, give me time! I loaned your sweater to a girl friend, and I just now got her on the phone. She'll bring it back in the morning."

Sally (13) had stolen things for years, and had just come back from Juvenile Hall where she had been taken for being found with stolen goods. The first day she was back at home, her mother's new hairdryer disappeared. Her mother was sure Sally had given or traded it to her friends, but had no hard evidence for this and knew Sally would deny it if confronted. We suggested that the mother announce to the family (which included three other girls) that she was upset by the loss of her hairdryer and that, in order to take care of herself, she would use the grocery money to buy another hairdryer, keeping enough money to buy plenty of bread but nothing else for the family. She was to explain that although she didn't at all like going on bread and water or putting the rest of the family on it, she preferred that to letting her inner being be injured without anything being done to take care of it.

Sally's mother didn't get her hairdryer back but she did experience a gratifying feeling of satisfaction and accomplishment in having, for almost the first time, stood up for herself. She also noticed that Sally's sisters, in addition to complaining about the unfairness of the situation, did have a lot to say to Sally about it. In the months that followed, Sally's mother persisted and, though the going was tough for a while, things eased up greatly for her.

We have been talking about what to do if your kid steals from you. A kid's stealing from brothers or sisters is another matter. If this happens, you will be strongly tempted to become the family judge again and settle the dispute, probably by scolding or punishing the miscreant. Don't. Empathize with the one who was stolen from if you wish, and say that you know he or she has what it takes to deal with the matter. You are helping your kid more by giving this sort of message than by moving heaven and earth to get some belonging back for him or her. The wronged kid will figure out how to handle the situation if you stay out of it.

● Saying worrisome or frightening things, name calling, swearing.

Included in this category are such things as:

Saying I don't love him.
Calling me bad names.
Whenever we have a fight, threatening to burn down the house.
Using foul language.
Saying she'll run away.
Saying she's going to kill herself.
Saying he'll blow our heads off tonight while we're asleep.

These are all things kids *say*. Generally, they say them to their parents for one of two reasons:
1. Because something is a real problem; the kid means what he or she says and wants help in dealing with it.
2. Because it gets a rise out of the parent.
If your kid's talk is for the first reason, it would be best for you to do something effective about it. If it's for the second, it would be best if you put your attention elsewhere. In neither case would it be helpful for you to give negative attention by becoming upset, hitting, shouting back, or feeling worried, guilty, frustrated, or angry about it.

Therefore, we recommend that the first time or two any of these things is said, you take it seriously, express your concern, and offer to help. Further, if what your kid says seems to you to imply a real danger, do what you can to avert it—perhaps by notifying the police, or by taking your kid to a mental hospital for an evaluation. For example, the parents of the boy who said he would blow their heads off called in the police. We also asked them to remove the gun they had in the house. The parents whose son said he would burn the house down offered to pay for counseling if he wanted it, and they also called the police.

Then, once you've taken these reasonable precautions, if your kid continues to say things like this without making an effort to solve the problem, we'd start considering him or her to be blackmailing: that is, using words to egg you into giving negative attention by getting upset or to get you to back down on some stand you have taken. Our basic recommendation: use the assertive techniques of the next chapters, but *first make sure you're not encouraging these remarks by the way you react to them*. Stop allowing yourself to become upset every time the kid says something like this.

Often when we see a parent bothered by what a kid is saying, it seems to us there's a bullfight going on and the parent is being the bull. We've often wished we could whisper a few words to bulls in real bullfights, in which the bull has the power and the matador controls it. He needs only flick a small red flag to make the bull become upset, roar, and come thundering at him in a charge. No doubt the bull believes that his problem is the matador, or at least the red flag; however, as we see it, his problem is his own readiness to get upset and charge every time the matador wants him to and gives him the signal to do so. We'd like to tell the bull:

Try not charging.

You're feeding right into this person's ploys by turning on an upset everytime he waves a flag. Think of how foolish he would feel if he couldn't make you do it! He would suddenly be the one with a problem.

Your adrenalin is precious. Take care of it; hoard it; don't pour it out so recklessly in anger or worry at someone else's signal. Keep your adrenalin dry!

Please consider whether there is any way in which you've been overreacting to things your kids say. Decide that whatever you do from now on when your kid says things like this, you will not turn on your anger, worry, guilt, frustration, nor begin shouting, hitting, or crying, when he or she gives the signal. Don't be a bull.

We once observed a perfect example of a kid being manipulated in this way by another kid. Read it and ask if by any chance you have been reacting as Peter did in the following situation:

> Carol (10) and Peter (9) had got into an argument of the,
> "It is so!" "It is not!" "It is so!" variety. When they were
> well into it, Carol's responses gradually became shorter
> and shorter ("It is!" and then merely, "Is!") while Peter,
> insisting that she shut up entirely, gave more and more
> furious and complicated answers ("It is not, you stupid!").
> Soon he began hitting the walls and stamping the floor in
> helpless rage. In the end, Carol sat lazily on her bed and
> needed give only the tiniest of squeaks in whatever timing
> she wished to send Peter into a frenzy of screams.

Clearly in this case the issue was no longer the particular
thing the two kids were arguing about, but rather one person's discovering how to get a rise out of another one.
Peter apparently never figured out that he was being turned
on and off by someone else, and that his outbursts weren't
getting him anything he wanted.

> Ernie (9) and Bob (12) had their mother and their new, very
> earnest, stepfather frantic. When pressed to say exactly
> what the boys did to achieve this, the parents could hardly
> define it, and finally pinned it down to things the boys said.
> It appeared that whenever either parent tried to set a limit
> (asking Ernie or Bob to help out, to go to bed, to make
> less noise, and so on) the boys would say, "You can't make
> me," "I don't like it here; I'm going to call my father
> and have him come get me," or, they would laugh. These
> things, especially the low, teasing laugh, drove the step-
> father wild. He had worked himself into a state of nervous
> tension and, literally, high blood pressure after several
> months of this situation. It seemed clear that by taking
> what the boys said so seriously and by becoming so upset
> over it, he was encouraging their verbal teasing.
>
> Among other things, we asked these parents to call
> the boys on all threats that they would phone their father
> ("You're welcome to use this phone to call your Dad, and
> meanwhile I want less noise around here.") We also asked
> them to hear what the boys said more as the chatter of
> small children than as momentous statements that could
> make a grown man helpless. It was not appropriate for a

worthwhile and bighearted man like this stepfather to let himself be provoked by these insignificant teasings.

One more word on the name-calling and swearing: If either of these is a problem for you, there's another step we would recommend before you move on to the next chapter.

Make sure you are not triggering these behaviors by doing them first.

Think carefully back to exactly what you said to your kid just before you got the last few instances of these items. Was it something derogatory or critical, or even a name, like, "Stupid!" "Dummy!" or "Fatso?" Did you swear first? Or did you give orders? Ask a question? Make a complaint? Did what you said have the word "you" in it? These are all triggers, and by becoming aware of them you could gain some control over the distressing things your kid is saying. You can probably turn on his or her problem talk by using these triggers, and decrease it by doing something different.

Ask yourself this question: "If I *wanted* to get my kid to swear or call me names, how would I do it?" Your answer to this may describe how you *are* doing it.

● Having a sullen or belligerent attitude.

Bernice (16) has a sullen attitude. She always looks gloomy and ill at ease.

Timothy (14) has a belligerent attitude. He makes a gesture that makes me think he's going to hit me whenever I tell him something.

Tommy (15) sort of cringes and sneaks through the living room as if he thinks I'm going to hit him. I never have, and it makes me feel like the big monster.

If you're like us, you'll perceive a message behind these attitudes. It will seem to you that through these attitudes your kid is saying to you:

You're no good.

I'm unhappy and it's your fault.

You'd better watch out and treat me with kid gloves or you'll get hurt.

Please don't hit me, you childbeater!

Understanding these messages so well may be the way you invite your kid to keep up attitudes like these. We suggest you become much more dense. If you think there may be a real problem behind your kid's attitude, offer to help out if you can—once. After that we suggest you refuse to understand these subtle attitudinal messages, and trust that if your kid has real trouble and wants to bring it up with you, he or she will say something straight out.

Think over the attitude problem in the following way:

First, make sure you're not triggering your kid's unpleasant attitude by being bossy, or saying derogatory things, or looking at the kid in a disapproving or angry or disappointed way yourself. In short, make sure *your* attitude is one of friendly courtesy.

If the attitude makes you feel afraid, as a belligerent attitude sometimes does, decide what you'll do if worse comes to worst and you actually do get hit, for instance— and then relax in the knowledge that you know just how you will act and so need not make any decisions about it. Once you've made this decision, fail to notice the belligerent gestures. In other words, if you're actually getting hit, do something effective for yourself, such as calling the police. If you're not, firmly drop the problem. Refuse to take the third alternative, of living in fear and worry about something you can't control.

Finally, check to see what you've been doing when you noticed the attitude—that pang of worry, guilt, anger, or fear you experience. That's your part in reinforcing the attitude you don't like. Decide to turn on any other response instead of one of these feelings. If it fits your life style, you might gear yourself up to run after the kid to tickle him or her every time you notice the cringing, or the gloom, or the abused look.

Sometimes parents reinforce unpleasant attitudes like these by taking them personally—by seeing the kid's attitude as aimed directly at the parent. Thus if a son or daughter takes on a sad or sullen look, or says "Good morning" in a low voice, the parent thinks this has something to do with him or her, and feels accused somehow. Now, this may be a completely accurate perception; your kid may actually be feeling something negative toward you. It may also be a faulty perception; he or she may not be thinking of you at all, but simply have a sore toe or be half asleep. Whichever the case, for you to perceive the attitude as directed toward you is a mistake, because doing so gets you something you don't want; it locks the attitude, encourages it to keep happening. Try instead letting it be OK whatever attitude your kid has, so long as it does not directly injure you. You might decide that it's all right for each person in a family to have a different attitude. There could be a cheerful, a sullen, a grave and determined, and a cranky one in your family—and as long as no one's being hurt, the variety in attitude could enrich the whole family.

After all, we see that different nations of the world tend to encourage different life styles. The people of one nation tend to be frank and open; other peoples are known as more gloomy, or reserved, or volatile, or polite. Every one of these is a valid life attitude for a human being. You could let it be OK that your kid has what seems to you a gloomy, a sullen, or a hostile attitude.

Harry (13) was a quiet, restrained boy who spoke very little. His stepmother was an open, highly expressive person herself, and it always seemed to her that Harry's silent, rather dour expression meant that things were going wrong for him and that it was her fault somehow. She had done many kindly things to win him over, but his silence, his gloomy looks, and especially the way he said "Good morning" to her (like a robot, she felt) made her think he was antagonistic to her. She may have been right; what she did not see was that her anxious focus on Harry's attitude was locking that attitude in place, and that Harry may simply have had a different personal style from hers.

- Abusing favors a parent has granted.

Let's consider one more set of problems that parents sometimes encourage by almost asking for them to happen. The following items seem to us like instances in which the kid is abusing favors the parent has implicitly or explicitly granted.

Borrows my car and doesn't take good care of it.
Borrows money and doesn't return it.
Uses my make up and leaves it a mess.
Leaves my tools out to be ruined.
Doesn't show up at the appointed place and time when I go to pick her up.
Doesn't return his library books and leaves me to pay the fine.
Orders me to take him here and there; doesn't ask courteously.

These items are alike in that almost any outsider would see that in a sense the parent is asking for the misbehavior, while the parent is aware only of feeling frustrated, ill-treated, helpless, angry. We've been in this position ourselves and still feel amazed at how blind we were to the fact that we were *permitting* the misbehavior.

One of our sons drove our car carelessly. He backed it into a pole, denting the rear fender, and declined to fix it. We were excited, upset, angry. He drove it carelessly again and ran it into a dirt pile, smashing the front grill. We were upset and scolded him. Yet a third time, he drove it hard and fast without oil until it broke down, a total wreck. Throughout all of this it never occurred to us that we were giving him permission to use our car and that *we didn't have to.*

Do you do this sort of thing? If your kid doesn't return money he or she has borrowed from you, have you continued to lend more before it's made right for you? If your kid leaves your tools out, do you permit him or her to use them again before you feel good about it? If your kid misuses your car, or your library card, or your typewriter, or any personal belonging of yours, do you continue to let him or her use it after the first time? If so, your permitting these things may be one of the triggers in bringing about the misbehavior. By granting a favor after it's been abused and when nothing has been done to make it right, you invite your kid to continue abusing it.

All of these are items that happen again and again, and their basic pattern is this:

1. Your kid presses for some favor—either asks for it or simply takes it for granted (to use your car, to be picked up, to use your library card).

2. You grant it, either by giving direct permission or by simply not saying no.

3. The kid abuses the favor, but also expects it again.

4. You feel abused, mistreated, frustrated, angry— and yet you grant the same favor again.

This pattern is based on some ideas in both your kid's head and yours. They are ideas like these:

A parent belongs to his or her kid.
A parent has no rights and must not be so selfish
  as to claim anything for him or herself.
A good parent is one who is ready to give him or
  herself over to the kid.

Having these ideas, the parent does give him or herself over, begins to feel natural resentment at being taken for granted, and then is liable to feel wrong and guilty for even feeling resentful.

Your continuing to agree to the favor *triggers* the misbehavior, and your failing to take care of yourself when it's been abused *reinforces* it.

The basic skill we recommend you learn in order to deal with being taken advantage of is that of *Refusing Favors.* Here's how to go about it.

First, think for a moment of all the different ways in which your particular kid presses you for something. How does he or she say it?

Hey Mom, we're out of bread.
Dad, wake me up at seven, will you?
Dad, you can pick me up at the movie at 12:30
Can I borrow $5?
Mom, take me to the bike shop.
Dad, I'm taking the car tonight.
May I have a dog?
I'm bringing home a dog.
Am I going to have to drive that old clunker of yours when I get my driver's license?
I want a new Datsun for my graduation present.

These are all situations in which, if you say yes to your kid, you're doing a favor. These are not things you owe to him or her; they're favors. And because they're favors, you can appropriately feel free to say yes or no to them.

As you think of these examples, notice whether you feel you *have* to say yes, or if your first impulse is to jump to take care of the request, without first considering whether you really want to or not. If you're doing this, you probably feel that it's your job to wait on your kid, and your kid may well feel it's his or her right to be waited on.

Notice that many of these are requests you might want to say yes to if the relationship with your kid were going well, and that you might resent if you were feeling unfairly treated in general. For example, "Hey Mom, we're out of bread" sounds good coming from a cheerful kid who's just finished his or her part of the dishes; it grates coming in a demanding tone from a kid who's done nothing but munch out in front of the TV all day while you've been doing your work. In the latter case, you may well feel like saying no. And certainly if the request has a negative history behind it, if it's in an area in which your kid has repeatedly abused your permissiveness, something in you will want to refuse, and probably will keep wanting to refuse until things are made right for it.

> If Dave hasn't showed up when you've gone to pick him up in the past, you won't want to go pick him up next time.

> If Sheila borrowed money from you before and didn't return it, something in you will want not to lend her any next time.

> If Carl has wrecked your car, or if you discover he's been trying to see whether it will do 100, or if he never refills the gas tank, you may well want to say no the next time he asks for it.

> If Linda didn't take care of her fish, you may want not to get her a dog when she asks.

Our point is that every time your kid makes a request or a demand, something in you will know very well whether it *wants* to agree or not. In the past you may always have said yes because you thought somehow that you had to. From now on, whenever your kid asks for something, *focus your attention on your inner signal-giver; find out whether it wants to say yes or no, and then follow its wishes.* This means that sometimes, probably when your kid is pleasant to be with and you're feeling good about him or her, you will want to say yes, and you will do so. And at other times, you will refuse. Here's how to do the refusing.

First, if you're going to change what you do about favors, it's fair to let your kid know that things will be different. Therefore tell him or her once, in an I-statement, what you plan to do. It can be short and sweet, and you can do it in a relaxed and kindly way.

> Jackie, I'm dissatisfied with the fact that I sometimes say yes to favors when I really don't want to. I'm going to take care of myself and do favors for

you only when I feel good about it, when I really want to.

Now, relax and go about your life—until the next request comes up.

As soon as it does, STOP! Resist the urge to say yes without even thinking about it, and instead, ask yourself whether you *want* to grant it. If the answer is no, say to your kid in a gentle and relaxed tone:

No.

Then add the most honest and short I-statement reason you can think of for your not wanting to say yes.

Janet: You can pick me up at the pizza palace.
Dad: No, Janet. I feel uncomfortable about the way I was asked.

Joe (at a restaurant): Mom, can I have your dessert?
Mother: No, Joe. I want it myself.

Jeff: I'm taking the car tonight.
Father: No, Jeff. I feel uneasy about your driving my car.

Burt: (whose father had agreed to pay him $5 for washing the car): Can I have my $5 in advance?
Father: No. I feel nervous wondering whether I'm going to get my side of the bargain.

Bill: Take me to the bike shop now.
Mother: No. I don't want to.

Marian: Mom, I need to take your camera to school for an assignment.
Mother: No. I don't like to lend my camera.

You may be tempted to pad your "No" with extra explanations.

No, Joe, I'm hungry, and I especially like this kind of dessert, and you already had yours, and it's not polite to ask for someone else's dessert, and besides, it has coconut in it and you don't like that.

Don't do it. Stick to your short, direct I-statement. The extra verbiage only muffles it. Don't give any other reasons, either. Reasons are appropriate for times when you're on good terms with your kid and would really like to say yes but have some compelling reason not to, so you explain why you're saying no instead. We're talking here about times when something in you feels it's being walked on, and does not want to say yes. In this case, giving extra reasons only tells everyone that you do not feel you have a right to say no. Especially avoid the temptation to give reasons that aren't based on your own wants for yourself. For example, "No, Joe, you know dessert will give you pimples." Simply give your own personal reason, concisely, and then stop.

Your kid may respond in any way from a cheery "OK" to a screaming tantrum; you may get no pressure at all to change your mind or you may get a great deal.

Once you've given your no, it's important to stand firm unless you honestly change your mind about wanting to grant the favor. If there's pressure to give in, listen quietly to what your kid says or does, and then repeat your refusal courteously:

No, I don't want to.

No, I don't lend my camera out.

No, I want it myself.

We've now mentioned five problem behaviors that parents often invite. At this point, please look over the remaining items on your parent's-life list to see if you might have been triggering or reinforcing them in the past.

Have you been triggering the behavior before it starts by:

Using "you's"?
Asking questions?
Giving orders?
Complaining?
Making derogatory remarks?

Doing basically the same kind of thing you complain of in your kid, yourself, first?

Setting the situation up in some way that makes the behavior more likely?

Have you been reinforcing the behavior after it happens by giving negative attention:

Scolding? Punishing? Lecturing? Weeping?

Experiencing unpleasant emotions—anger, fear, worry, frustration?

Becoming upset? Glum? Anxious?

Use this chapter to figure out how you will, from now on:

Use I-statements when you're talking about anything that bothers you.

Set up the things in your life in such a way as to make them convenient and comfortable for you, without encouraging others to steal from you, take advantage of you, and so on.

Decide upon how you will behave when troublesome items occur—in ways that do not include giving negative attention.

If parent's-life items continue to be a problem after you've sincerely stopped any triggering or reinforcing of them, go on to the assertive techniques of the next chapters. You'll be in a sound position to use them because you'll know you're not encouraging your kid to misbehave at the same time as you press him or her to do better.

The only way we can see in which you might still be asking for these parent's-life items is by the old, well-known response we call *putting up with it*, and we'll be working on ways to change this next.

Eight

Standing Up for Yourself

If you've sincerely worked through the first seven chapters of this book, then at this point:

You value your kid's decision-making ability and are encouraging him or her to make the decisions that affect his or her own life. You are out of trying to control your kid's life, if you ever were.

As much as possible, you are being a friend, wanting to see your kid be happy in his or her own way. You see your kid as competent and as able to run his or her own life, and you're interested to see how he or she does it.

You have stopped any triggering or reinforcing of your kid's troublesome behavior.

You are pleasant and courteous to your kid, and you are continuing to provide a home and all the support that goes with it.

If you are doing these things, it seems to us that you are certainly respecting your kid's "rights." You are being fair and considerate and are not asking for mistreatment in any obvious way. If you're still having problems, then, it would seem that you are being treated unfairly, that *your* rights are not being respected. It's time to stand up for them.

Doing that can be one of the most rewarding enterprises in this book. It can bring about a much improved relationship with your kid, a better feeling about yourself, some tense moments and some wonderful, exhilarating ones —and it can be fun. We hope you enjoy it all.

This part of the work is most effective with clear parent's-life items—things which, if a room mate of yours did them, would lead almost anyone to agree that you were being treated unfairly. It applies to items like these:

Makes messes and doesn't clean them up.
    Leaves his wet towels all over the bathroom.
    Leaves the kitchen a mess.
    Leaves her dirty dishes all over the family room.
    Doesn't clean up his dog's messes.
Doesn't take care of her dog.
Continues to steal your things.
Plays loud stereo at all hours.
Stays out past a reasonable in-time and then breaks windows, locks, etc., getting in.
Racks up long distance phone bills without either asking your permission or paying you.
Freeloads—lives with you and will neither go to school, work, nor contribute in any other way.
Won't do chores.
Brings kids into your house while you're gone.
Has parties in the house while you're at work, perhaps during school hours, perhaps involving alcohol, drugs, sex.
Grows marijuana in the house, or stores it in his room, putting you in an illegal position.
Persists in smoking in bed, even after burning holes in bedclothes and furniture.
Knocks holes through plaster and doors, dents refrigerators, breaks tables and other furniture, when angry.
Your pregnant daughter moves her boyfriend in to live without asking your permission (or your son moves his pregnant girlfriend in).

Aspects of kid's-life items that you held in reserve because they do affect you directly are appropriate here too.

Please plan to spend some weeks, perhaps a month or two, making the shift into standing up on these items. We're aiming toward quite a basic change in your attitude—from feeling obligated and duty-bound about your kid to feeling comfortable about taking care of yourself. That won't be achieved by going at it in a hurry, by suddenly throwing out a few assertive statements and then settling back into old ways. It is, rather, a slow, thoughtful, and persistent working at the steps, one after the other, that will do the job.

Look over your parent's-life list and pick an item at about middle range for you. We're going to take you through a series of escalating steps to use in dealing with this item. In the process of doing this you will learn a philosophy and technique for dealing with all of the parent's-life items on your list. The particular item you work on may resolve itself at any point along these steps, but it need not matter to you which step does it because you know you're going to stick to it until the problem is resolved for you.

The five major steps will be:

1. Establishing the fairness of what you want. This step will include an honest attempt to negotiate with your kid; whether or not this succeeds, at the end of this step you will have made a clear statement of what you want.
   The problem may be solved at this point. If not, you move on to Step Two.

2. Standing firm for your want against your kid's pressure to give in.

3. Repeating Step Two several times if the problem recurs. It is most likely that the problem will resolve itself here. However, if it does not, you go to Step Four.

4. Establishing credibility in your word, to prove you will

do what you say you will do to get your rightful due.

5. A parental strike.

We will use as our main example in going through the steps the kid's failure to contribute to the work load in the family. However, the approach we describe for this item applies for all of the parent's-life items. As you get experience with applying these principles to the first of the items on your parent's-life list, extend exactly the same procedure to the remaining items. Most parent's-life problems reduce to quite manageable proportions or disappear altogether when you conscientiously go through the first four of these steps. For those problems that don't it is appropriate to consider, as a last resort, the fifth and final step, the parental strike. We will talk about this in Chapter 9.

Suppose, then, that you're feeling unfairly treated because your teenage kid does not, will not, "forgets" to, do anything to help out around the house.

Step One

First, to establish a sound basis for your campaign on this item, establish the fairness of what you want. This step may take some new communication skills on your part, so be sure to read the whole step over before you begin working on it.

This step is important because, although it may seem obvious to you that you are being unfairly treated, it is quite possible that your kid believes he or she has a *right* to treat you in this way, or even that this is the way you *want* it. Now, it has been found that in any sort of encounter, the side that everyone knows is in the right has a tremendous advantage. You may have noticed, with animals, that even a small dog can chase a big one out of its yard— because both dogs know the small one is "right."

Studies show that when two equally strong stickleback fish have a conflict, the fish who is guarding its own nest and therefore is in the "right" *always* wins.

Your aim in this step, then, is simply to establish in your own and your kid's minds the fairness and thus the rightness of what you want. Since the parent's-life items are all things in which almost everyone in our society would agree you're being treated unfairly, you can expect that something in your kid, too, will recognize the fairness of your want, if you present it in a non-accusing way. From then on, if your kid repeats the misbehavior, he or she has to feel, not like a glamorous rebel against authority, but like someone who is doing an injustice. That doesn't feel nearly so good.

Don't count on your kid's behavior changing much as a result of this step. However, when you're finished with this step, you will have stated clearly what you think is fair, and your kid will either have agreed or disagreed with your view of fairness or will have refused to talk about it with you. It makes little difference which happens, because the kid is likely to misbehave again in any case, but you will have established your concept of fairness, and that gives you a sound basis for taking the next steps.

Here's an effective way to carry out this step.

Pick a time when you and your kid are reasonably relaxed, and in a courteous, friendly voice make a three-sentence announcement that *you are dissatisfied with the situation*, that *you want to see it changed*, and that *you would like the kid's help with it*. All three sentences should begin with "I" and only the third sentence should have any "you" or "your" in it. They could go something like this:

Sentence 1. John, I'm feeling dissatisfied with:

the way the work load has been distributed around here.

(or, depending upon the item you have picked to work on:)

what's happening with the dog messes.

the way my clothes have been disappearing.

finding people have been in the house while I'm gone.

hearing so many four-letter words around here.

so much noise from the stereo.

Sentence 2. I want a change in the situation so that it's more fair.

(or)

I definitely want a more fair arrangement in this matter.

Sentence 3. I'd like your feedback on how I could solve it.

(or)

I'd like some help from you in working out a change.

I'd appreciate any help you could give me on this.

I'd be interested, if you have any suggestions that could help out.

Your kid's response will either suggest to you some readiness to talk about it, to begin making a deal, or it will make you feel put off. If it sounds to you like a readiness to talk, begin working on a deal. It might go as it did for Carl's mother:

Mother: Carl, I'm dissatisfied with the way our house is always so messy and my feeling that I'm the only one who works on it. I want a more fair arrangement. I'd like some help from you in working out a change.

Carl: I don't like the house being so messy either. (Occasionally kids do say things like this).

Mother: I'd like some help in setting up a better arrangement. (Stick to your subject: getting a more fair deal).

Carl: Well, I won't be so messy from now on.

Mother: (consulting her own signal-giver) I want something more definite than that. I'd be willing to make dinners and clean the kitchen if you'd clean the living room and bathroom every week.

Carl: If I have to, I'd rather do the kitchen than the bathroom.

Mother: I'd feel good about that.

If your kid responds to your first three sentences in this way, congratulate yourself. You've just got a verbal agreement on what would be fair. You're perhaps more likely, though, to get a response that makes you feel put off. When you give your three sentences your kid may try to shift the subject of the conversation from your wish for a more fair arrangement to something else, such as who gets the place dirty in the first place, or the fact that the vacuum is broken, or anything else to sidetrack you. Or he or she may simply walk out on you, or call you a name, or just grunt, or hang his or her head and look embarrassed. If any of this happens, simply keep pressing toward a deal by repeating variations of Sentence 3.

I'd really like your help on this.

I want some ideas on how I might solve this problem.

If, after three or four repetitions you still get nothing that sounds like cooperation, continue to repeat variations of Sentence 3 and begin adding preliminary negotiating offers, still as I-sentences.

I'd be willing to make dinner every night if you'd take over the yard work.

I'd feel good about it if you'd take care of keeping the living room cleaned up.

I'd feel OK if I could count on three hours of solid work from you every Saturday.

Or, if you're working on a different item:

I'd feel good about the dog if I knew you'd clean up the messes.

I'd be willing to have the stereo on two hours in the evening if I could count on quiet the rest of the time.

Make your statement, wait to see what the response is, and if it's another put-off, simply repeat some variation of your statement again.

Take your time at this: talk in a slow and relaxed way. Every time you make a fair and courteous statement like this and wait, there is a pressure on your kid to respond, so let that pressure work. You might wait a full fifteen seconds between statements.

If you keep at it in this way, quietly and politely, ignoring for the moment any of your kid's attempts to distract you and simply sticking to your statements, your kid may eventually give you some response showing willingness to make a deal with you. For example:

Dave: Well, what do you want *me* to do about it? (Never mind your kid's tone of voice. Stick to getting a verbal agreement if possible).

Parent: I'd feel good if the front lawn were kept up.

Dave: I won't do slave work like that! (Never mind how reasonable or unreasonable your kid's remarks are. Stay focussed on setting up a fair arrangement).

Parent: I want to be able to count on a fair share being done by everyone in the family.

Dave: Why don't you get Sis to do her share? (Never mind diversionary remarks like this; stick to getting an agreement).

Parent: I'd feel better if the dinners were cooked, or the ironing done.

Dave: Oh... (four letter word)! I'll take the ironing then. (Never mind swearing and a reluctant tone at this time. Stick to getting the verbal agreement).

Parent: I'd feel good about that.

If after fifteen or twenty minutes your kid still won't even talk about what would be fair, or if he or she simply leaves the room or outright refuses to talk with you, then drop the subject for the moment, and be ready to repeat the whole step again in a few hours or the next day. *Make three such attempts*—more, if you want to—before you decide that your kid is not going to help you solve this problem. When you reach this point and feel you've given him or her ample chance to come up with something, then state clearly, once, what you think would be fair, and hence what you will expect, and then stop. Stay with I-statements and put in as few "you's" as possible when you say this.

I think it would be fair if I counted on you to take care of the living room every week, and that's what I'm going to do.

I think it would be fair if I shopped for the groceries and paid for them and could count on you to bring them in and put them away. That's what I'll expect to happen.

I think it would be fair if I knew that either you were getting yourself educated, or were paying room and board, or were taking charge of the work around the house. I'll look for one of those to happen.

I think it would be fair if anything that gets broken around here is paid for, and I'll expect that.

If you've managed to get some sort of verbal agreement on your kid's part, finish up this step in a similar way by making one, clear, summary statement of what you will expect.

I'll make the dinners, then, and I'll count on having the living room and the kitchen cleaned.

I'll do my part, then, and I'll count on having the

ironing done every week.

I'll count on having no one but you in the house while I'm out, then.

I'll expect anything that gets broken to be paid for, then.

I'll be looking for freedom from stereo, then, except between 9 and 11 P.M.

If you've really carried this step through sincerely, you will know at this time that you have established for everyone that you are fair, direct, and want a solution to this problem. You've also served a fair warning of what you expect. There's a bare possibility that simply doing this much will resolve the problem for you. Whether it does or not, though, you've still advanced your cause, because you have chosen the ground on which the encounter with your kid will occur, and it's one in which it's clear that *you're in the right*.

From now on, if you stand really firm, your kid may very well want to agree with you, and if you can make it possible for him or her to do so without losing face or pride, the situation may go well.

In any case, after you've made your summary announcement, read over Step Two so that you'll be fully prepared for the next move. Prepare the short sentence we ask you to make in that step and store it in your memory. Then forget about the problem until you get the next zing about this item. Pay no attention to whether the kid does the job or not. If he or she does do the job, pay no attention to the methods he or she uses. Do not check to see whether the job has been done, and do not remind your kid. Rather, keep your attention on enjoying your own life, and as long as you are feeling comfortable, do nothing about the item.

Sometime, a few hours or a few days after you've stated what you want, your enjoyment and comfort is likely to be interrupted by the old, familiar zing about this item.

If your kid's job was to help with the work for a

couple of hours on Saturday mornings, you will realize that he or she is already out of the house for the day with the work undone, and you'll *feel a zing.*

If your kid's job was to care for the yard, you'll glance out the window, notice the leaves are only half raked and the garden tools have been left lying out, and you'll *feel a zing.*

If you've said you will expect no other kids in the house while you're out, you'll see evidence that kids have been in the house, and you'll *feel a zing.*

If you've said you'd count on freedom from stereo except in the evening, you'll hear a loud blast in the middle of the day, and you'll *feel a zing.*

If you've said you'll expect your kid's dog to be fed, you'll notice the dog is still hungry past its feeding time, and you'll *feel a zing.*

(If you notice that the job is not done and you do not feel a zing, but instead for some reason feel OK about it—do nothing! Your task is not to see that your kid does the job—rather, your task is to take care of your zings. If you don't get a zing when you see the job isn't done, then presumably you're comfortable about things, and there's no problem. In short, we ask you to let the zing, not the item itself, be your guide in proceeding.)

As soon as you feel a definite zing because the item you're working on has happened again, move on to Step Two—*standing firm for your want against pressure from your kid to back down.*

Step Two

The primary purposes of Step Two are to get practice in persisting and in avoiding being sidetracked. Accomplishing these two things will make your Step Two effort a success whether or not you get your rightful want at this point.

Here is what to do for Step Two.

Prepare ahead of time a short, clear I—statement describing what you will want to have happen to ease your zing if the want you described in Step One is not met. *Make sure there is no "you" in the statement.*

If the item is failure to do a job, then say:

I'd like the kitchen cleaned up.

I want some solid help this morning.

I'm wanting the dog mess cleaned up.

If the item is something that really can't be made up because it's already happened, then say:

I'd like to know no one is coming in the house without my permission.

I want to know I won't hear any four letter words around here.

If your kid has "borrowed" something of yours without asking, then say:

I'd like my blouse back just as it was (laundered and ironed) and I want to know no one is going into my closet without asking me.

Or:

I want any dog in my house to be taken care of.

I'd like the money for this phone bill.

I want my house free of pot.

I'd like the hole in the wall repaired.

When you have designed your statement, memorize it and hold it ready to use.

Now realize that in this matter you are standing up for a fair and essentially equal-rights arrangement between the two of you, and your kid needs to have you persevere in claiming this arrangement. However, he or she also needs to know you can and will be firm in taking care of yourself in this way, and it's part of the game for the kid to give you some resistance to test that firmness. Your kid may throw you all sorts of hooks designed to pull you off the track and turn the conversation to something other than your want. Your job will be to keep your part of the conversation firmly on your want and resist all the tempting side issues your kid will bring up.

You will start this conversation on the subject of *your* want; be determined that no other subject, no matter how important it may be at other times, will pull you away from your want until it has been satisfied.

Be prepared to address your entire body to the task when you state your want. Don't call from the next room, or make your statement over your shoulder. Go to where your kid is, get fairly close (three to five feet) and let your whole body face your kid as you talk.

The very next time you see your kid after you experience the zing, go to him or her and make a *polite request*. This is probably the only question we'll ever recommend you ask your kid, and it has a purpose—not to get the kid to cooperate (it probably won't do that) but to lay a good base for the dialogue which will follow. It reminds the kid that you feel you have a right, that you are courteous, and that you will continue to take care of yourself.

Barbara, will you please clean up the kitchen?

Dan, will you please take care of the yard?

Megan, will you please put my mind at ease about whether you'll be going to school or paying room and board?

Joe, will you please feed the dog?

Steve, will you please pay me to cover this phone bill?

Your kid will make a response to your polite request that either makes you feel good, or leaves you still dis-

satisfied. If the response eases your zing and makes you
feel comfortable about the item, then simply give your kid
an I-message describing that comfortable feeling.

Dan: Oh, sure, Dad, I forgot all about it. I'll do
it right now.
Father: I'd like that.

Barbara: Oh, sorry 'bout that, Mom. I got busy with
something else, but the dishes will be done
within half an hour.
Mother: I feel good about that.

Megan: Oh, I forgot to tell you, Dad. I saw my school
counselor this morning and I'm starting back
to school with a full load on Monday morning.
Father: I'm glad to hear about that.

It's more likely that your kid's response will leave
you still feeling much of your zing, put off and doubtful
about whether the job is going to be done and your want
met. Your kid may say something like:

But I have to do my homework now.

OK, OK, I'll do it later!

It's not my turn.

How come I have to do all the dirty work?

or

I won't.

To heck with you! (or worse)

I'd pay you for the phone bill but I don't have any
money right now.

None of the classes I can get at school are any good.

These are all hooks designed to pull you away from the
subject of your want and into something else—into taking

responsibility for your kid's homework, into dropping the conversation, into arguing about turns, or about whether this is dirty work and why it need be done at all, into scoldings and counter-defiance and explanations, and so on. You've already given your kid a very fair chance to bring up problems like this, in Step One, and if they come up now, it's fair to ignore them. Refuse to be pulled into any of these other subjects, and instead: Begin responding to your kid by using the *three-part assertive sentence*.

The *first* part of the sentence is meant to let the kid know you heard him or her. It can have "you's" in it, because it is to be simply a reflection of what you heard your kid saying or expressing. To make this part of your sentence, simply listen to what your kid says or does, summarize it for yourself, and then give it back. You'll find that phrases such as, "I understand that...," "You're saying that...," and sometimes simply, "Mm hm," are good for beginning this part of the sentence.

I hear that you do have homework...

I understand you want to do it later...

You're saying it's not your turn...

You wonder why you have to do it...

You're saying you won't do it...

> or

I'm hearing that you don't have any money...

You don't like your classes...

The *second* part of the sentence is the word "and." You may find yourself wanting to use "but" instead. We find "and" to be more effective. In this sentence we're asking you to express two wants or feelings, your kid's and yours, and the word "but" connecting them implies that the two are in conflict and only one or the other is really valid. The word "and," on the other hand, implies that there are two wants and they can coexist. It bypasses any attempt to change this conversation into a conflict.

The *third* part of the sentence is the I-statement you have already prepared.

The total sentence, then, goes something like this:

(1)	(2)	(3)
I understand you want to do it later,	and,	I want the kitchen cleaned up.
You're saying it's not your turn,	and,	I want some solid help this morning.
You wonder why you have to do it,	and,	I want the dog mess cleaned up.

Your kid will probably respond with another hook; you handle it in the same way, simply reflecting it back to him or her, adding an "and," and then restating your basic I-statement. You can *keep your voice courteous and yourself comfortable* as you continue to respond in this way, because you don't have to put any energy into figuring out what to say (you already have your three-part pattern and your basic I-sentence) and you know that no matter how this particular incident turns out, you will continue to look after your want until it is satisfied. So you can't lose, and you are in a good position to remain calm and relaxed. You can let your kid do all the shouting, acting out, worrying, manipulating, and so on. This in itself is a tremendous change from the usual situation.

Be prepared for the many different kinds of hooks your kid may throw you. Here are some common ones we've heard, along with possible ways you might respond to them.

Your kid: You're always on my back!
You: You're saying I'm always on you about something—and—I'd like the kitchen cleaned up.

Your kid: You don't care about me!
You: I see you're thinking that I don't care about you —and—I'd like the kitchen cleaned up.

Your kid: Why do I have to do more than Sis?
You: Mm hm, you're wondering why Sis doesn't have to do more of the work—and—I'd like the kitchen cleaned up.

Your kid: You like her better than me!
You: I guess you're thinking I like her better—and—I'd like the kitchen cleaned up.

Your kid: I'm not going to do that slave work!
You: Mm hm, I understand you won't do slave work—and—I'd like the kitchen cleaned up.

Your kid: You're just saying what the counselor told you to!
You: Mm hm, you're hearing that I'm talking the way the counselor showed me—and—I want the kitchen cleaned up.

Notice that at this time:

    You need not answer questions.

    You need not justify your want.

    You need not prove you are fair, or that you care.

The job is simply to be loyal to your inner being by sticking with your want.

    If your kid walks out on you—stalks to his or her room, or runs out of the house—do not run after him or her, but simply go about your business until the next time the two of you meet. Then begin this new conversation by saying quietly: "Dan, I'd like the kitchen cleaned up."

    How long should you keep this up? Until you get a response *that eases your zing*—that is, that leaves you feeling reasonably assured your want will be cared for—or, until you've gone through your three-part sentence twenty times. Count on your fingers as you give the sentences; this may keep you feeling calm and just preoccupied enough that you do not get pulled into the well-designed hooks your kid can throw out to you.

If you go through this twenty times and your kid is still refusing to take care of your want, stop the three-part sentence. At this point drop your attention from your kid. Be especially sure you DO NOT GIVE YOUR KID ANY NEGATIVE ATTENTION WHATSOEVER. If you have feelings of discouragement or frustration now, turn them off, and allow yourself a feeling of satisfaction that you managed to give your three part sentence all twenty times. Now either do the job yourself or take steps to get it done in some other way. You can do this cheerfully, because if you've completed this step, it is a success—no matter how your kid responded and regardless of whether or not the job got done. Congratulate yourself, because you have stood up for your rights. Allow yourself to enjoy any feelings of confidence, even exhilaration, you may have experienced as you stood up in this way.

Step Three

Step Three is, essentially, to repeat Step Two the next time this same problem recurs.

Whether your original Step Two resulted in your kid's doing the job or not, you're likely to get the same old zing at least one more time. Again,

> You will walk through the kitchen, notice it is a mess, and *feel a zing*

> You will realize that someone has been in your house while you were away, and *feel a zing*.

> You will get a bill for a long distance phone call you didn't make, and you will *feel a zing*.

As soon as you feel this zing, remember that your job is to take care of it, and as your first step in doing so, turn to your kid and again make your polite request:

> "Barbara, will you please clean up the kitchen?"

You can count on the fact that your kid was not comfortable when you went through Step Two the first time. We find that people in general, adults as well as kids, feel very uncomfortable saying "No" to a fair, friendly, persistent statement like the one you made in Step Two. Even if your kid put on a cocky face and resisted your appeal through the whole twenty sentences, you can be certain that he or she did not enjoy it. When this second time comes up, it will dawn on your kid at about the second or third repetition of your sentence that that whole scene is about to repeat itself. Your kid is likely to think, "Oh, no, here we go again!" and may well opt to give you what you want gracefully rather than go through those uneasy and perhaps guilty feelings again—*if* you let him or her keep face doing it. That's one reason we ask you to stay courteous and relaxed, so the kid will know he or she won't get crowed over after agreeing to do what you want. Instead, you let the kid know how good it makes you feel to have your want taken care of:

Kid: I know, I know, I know; you want the kitchen cleaned! (going to do it)
You: I really feel good about your doing that.

You: ... and I do want the money for this phone bill.
Kid: Yeah, Dad, I hear you! I forgot to tell you about the call, but here's the money.
You: I'm glad, and so relieved you'll take care of it.

Repeat Step Two several times, depending upon (a) whether your kid shows any signs of being ready to take care of you, and (b) whether you've really followed Step Two instructions thoroughly and been courteous, friendly, persistent, throughout. If you can see ways in which you slipped up, repeat this step again and again. Do it until you're utterly comfortable going through it.

It's very likely that by the time you've gone through these three steps the situation with your kid will have improved noticeably. Most of the families we are able to help show the bulk of their improvement within a few weeks or even days after the parents honestly (1) let go trying to control the kid's-life items, as in Chapters 2 through 4, and (2) make a firm stand, as we've described, for their rights on the parent's-life items.

If doing everything we've suggested so far has made this kind of difference for you, your main job from now on will be to maintain the progress you have made. You can do that by following these two rules for yourself:

I will trust my kid to make his or her own decisions on kid's-life items.

Whenever I get a zing about a parent's-life item, I will do something to take care of it. My first step in that direction can be to tell my kid what I want, using the three-part assertive sentence.

We suggest that you read through the two steps still ahead in the following chapter. You may not actually have to use them, but knowing that you can and will if this is what it takes to take care of yourself can give you a worthwhile confidence. If you know with surety that you will stand up for yourself, it's far less likely that you will have to.

If your problem is still there after you've conscientiously gone through Steps 1, 2, and 3, we can think of two possible reasons. Both may be valid in your case. One is that you have not thoroughly enough followed through on the work of previous chapters, so that there is still too much intermixing of responsibility between you and your kid. You may still be struggling in some way to control the kid's-life items, and perhaps you are still seeing the kid as not able to make responsible decisions, or judging him or her, or feeling trapped yourself. If you have not taken care of these things, your kid may not feel like taking care of you on these parent's-life items.

If you think something like this might be happening, review the earlier chapters of this book, and give yourself time to get used to the philosophy they're based on. You may find the whole approach will work better for you a few months from now.

A second reason why these first three steps may not have changed the problem is that even now, *your kid may not believe you really will stand up for yourself.* Maybe you weren't firm and clear when you went through the steps, or maybe the kid is preoccupied with something else entirely and didn't get the point for that reason. Maybe he or she is getting so much safety out of being defined as the bad, irresponsible one that he or she can't or can't afford to see you as another, equal person with rights and needs of your own. In any case, it seems to us the kid is in danger of growing up with the idea that other people don't matter and that he or she has a right to be taken care of without making any return. That viewpoint won't serve the kid very well when he or she gets out in the world, and you may be doing him or her a real favor by going ahead with the next steps and giving your kid a chance to learn how to be an equal person.

Let's go ahead with the next steps, then, on the assumption that you have put a reasonable and sincere effort into the previous work in this book and that, for whatever reason, *your kid still has not caught on to the fact that you are a real person with feelings and wants of your own, and that you will take care of yourself.*

Nine

Following through

on Your Stand

You've now made a first, solid attempt to take care of yourself as far as these parent's-life items go. You did it by communicating to your kid as clearly as you could what you want. This attempt failed to solve the problem for you, and you are now left with the responsibility of finding some other way of taking care of yourself.

We'll take a slightly different direction in this chapter. We'll be asking you to take some physical actions and, later, to use those physical actions in taking care of yourself in relation to your kid. We emphasize again, as in earlier chapters, that taking care of yourself in this relationship will take care of your kid as well, in very important ways.

Before you begin Step Four, clear your mind for a shift to this new direction by doing a "Minnesota Fats."

Minnesota Fats was an aging billiard champion who had been engaged in a contest with an able, younger opponent for many hours. They'd been playing all night and at last, near morning, it appeared that neither of the exhausted, bleary eyed, grimy men would be able to win. It was apparently a deadlock. At this point, Minnesota Fats left the game to go to the washroom for a few moments. Calmly he washed his face and hands, wet and combed his hair, and put on a fresh shirt he had ready for the occasion. Then he returned to the game and, physically and mentally refreshed, won it within a few plays.

At this point, you're in somewhat the same situation Minnesota Fats was. You've been coping with this problem with your son or daughter for a long time. You just made a courageous stand which you hoped would solve that problem for you, and it didn't. The whole kid situation may seem deadlocked to you. Therefore, it's time for a Minnesota Fats break. Take it by getting yourself some time entirely away from the kid situation; spend it doing something you really enjoy, and keep at it until you've had at least a few hours during which you were so engrossed in having a good time that you didn't even think about your kid. Take a long, beautiful walk, or spend a day in the mountains, or visit friends for a few days or a few hours —whatever you like to do to clear your mind. Then, refreshed by this interlude, set your mind on the next steps we will be suggesting in working on the whole problem.

If, at this point in your work your kid still persists in doing things on your parent's-life list, he or she seems to be still wanting to exert power over you. And, evidently, he or she is able to do this through knowing what pushes your button and what you will do when it is pushed. You are predictable. Ironically, it is likely that one way in which you are predictable is that if your kid persists long enough and with enough unpleasantness, you will ultimately go along with his or her program just to get some peace. Step Four will be to establish an entirely new notion in your kid's mind, namely, that whatever you say, you will stick with regardless of his or her level of effort to get you to change. In other words, his or her old prediction about how you will act will fail.

We think it is very important to let your kid become acquainted with a new, somewhat unpredictable, you. Thus we urge you, before beginning the next step in this chapter, to *prepare yourself to have some fun becoming a generally more daring, unpredictable, spontaneous, and zany person than you have been.*

Up to now, the following statements have probably been true of what happens between you and your kid:

Your kid does the unmanageable, unpredictable, crazy things, and *you* have the role of worried, responsible one.

When you and your kid talk together, you both talk about and focus on what *your kid* is doing, what he or she wants, how he or she feels—and what *you* do, want, and feel, has little or no part in the conversation.

You worry about what your kid is going to do, and *your kid* does not worry about what *you* will do at all, because he or she sees you as a stable, entirely predictable person who is all figured out.

Let's reverse this at least in part, and get the two of you on a more equal basis.

Here is how we suggest that you do that.

Imagine that for many years you've been a prisoner in a chain gang. You've had the same duties in this gang for so long that you no longer even see the situation, the duties, the other prisoners, the fairness or unfairness of the way things are done, but simply operate on dull automatic, doggedly doing the tasks you think you have to do. Now imagine that suddenly you are set free. You're still in the same physical situation, but you're now free—to stay in this situation or to go, to do the same old tasks or to change to something new, to reassess your whole situation as a free person. As this free person, look around in your life now and begin speaking to yourself, over and over, in these sentences:

I'm free to do as I wish; what do I want to do right now—for the next five minutes?

Run?
Talk?

Lie down and rest?
Make up a little dance?
See how many colors I can see without changing
    position?
Nothing?

I'm free to do as I wish; what do I want to do for the next few weeks or months?

Buy a typewriter?
Play the stock market?
Lose twenty pounds?
Take up wood carving?

I'm free to do as I wish; what would I do if I were a bit zany?

Run about on all fours?
Change jobs?
Stay up all night listening to records?
Laugh?

As a very small child you undoubtedly had plenty of ideas about things you wanted to do. The ability to think as you did then is not lost; it's there to be used whenever you decide to tap into it again.

I'm free to do as I wish; what would I do right now if I were "five" years old?

Stretch up and see if I can touch the ceiling?
Run under the sprinkler and cool off?
Dive into deep snow in my bathing suit? (One of
    us did just that.)
Run away from my kids for a few days? (Yes,
    one of us did that too.)

Give yourself lots of leeway when you answer these questions—let the answers be as crazy as you can make them. Then pick some of the craziest and do them. It could go something like these examples we've invented:

You are Tony's mother and he comes home past 3 A.M. one night. He comes in as quietly as possible so he won't be caught and scolded with, "You were supposed to be home by twelve." "You're late." "Where have you been?" "You're grounded." As he opens the front door he is amazed to hear peppy Mexican music, and then to see you lying on the floor writing busily, surrounded by a litter of papers, empty coffee cups, and records. He blurts out, "What are you doing?" (close to the first time *he* has ever asked *you* what you were doing). "I've decided to stay up until I learn all the Spanish words to my records," you say.

You are driving your daughter to school, as you usually do on your way to work. At an intersection where you usually turn left, you turn right. Your daughter asks incredulously, "Where are you going, Dad?" (close to the first time *she* has ever asked *you* where you were going). You say, "I'm taking the River Road 'shortcut.' I've guessed the mileage and I want to see how close I come."

Your daughter Marcia has checked the bathroom door several times in the last half hour and notices that you are still in there. Finally she says, "Mom, what are you *doing* in there?" (close to the first time *she* has ever asked *you* why you're taking so long in the bathroom). You say, "I'm taking a bubble bath and eating a popcorn omelet I made."

These are all "a little bit crazy" things; we're asking you to do lots of them and, in fact, make a habit of doing them all the time. How many you do is limited only by your ability to think of them, and we have found that once you let yourself think of a few, they can start coming more and more easily. It's so much fun to do them, once you've begun, that it's easy to get into a habit of doing them, not just for your kid, but because they are fun, for you.

Your going "crazy" in this way acts to correct the balance in what's happening between you and your kid, so that:

At least part of the time, *you* do the unmanageable, unpredictable, zany things, leaving the role of worried, responsible one to your kid, if he or she wants it.

At least part of the time, when you and your kid talk together, you both focus on what *you* want, how *you* are doing, how *you* feel.

At least part of the time, *you* do no worrying at all. If there's any worrying going on, *your kid* does it—wondering what you will do next, because he or she begins to see you as an unpredictable person. As a human being, you always were unpredictable, but your kid didn't know it, and to find this out about you is one of the nicest things for him or her to learn. Your kid does not have you all figured out. As you will notice as you do this step, *neither do you*, and that's nice to find out about yourself, too.

You've already made a start at doing all this, in Chapter 5. There we asked you to get into a habit of consulting yourself on how you are feeling and what you'd like to do, or be, or have. We asked you to do some small, spontaneous, fun things and to express your inner signal giver by dropping out spontaneous I-sentences every once in a while during the day: "I feel," "I like," "I want," and "I'm going to."

Now it's time to upscale all of this. If you work at it seriously, you will find yourself becoming more and more free feeling with it, more and more comfortable talking in this way in front of your kid, and in front of his or her friends and, for that matter, in front of the neighbors, the people at the shopping center, and all of your relatives.

Notice that we're not asking you to do anything to hurt other people. We're simply asking that you yourself do things that will make *you* feel happier, freer, more confident that you can count on yourself to take care of your own wants.

When you've practised being more spontaneous and unpredictable enough to feel quite comfortable about it, add Step Four.

Step Four

In this step your job is to *establish the credibility of your word*, to prove to your kid that you will do what you say you will. In this step we're preparing for a confrontation and ultimatum, a parental strike, to be used if serious problems with your kid aren't resolved before things go that far. Well before that real ultimatum, it is vital that your kid believe that you will definitely do whatever you say you will. Only if your kid believes that can he or she believe you when you make a serious statement of your intention to "strike." If, when you give this ultimatum, the kid thinks that you do not mean it and that you may give in, he or she can play brinkmanship with you, and continue misbehavior just to see whether you mean it. On the other hand, if the kid knows very well it is truly an ultimatum, because *you always do what you say you will*, then he or she can make a responsible choice, either to go along with it, or to refuse it and take the consequences.

This step, then, is a pre-ultimatum move designed to establish in your kid's mind that you can be counted on to do what you say you will.

For this step, we ask you to do a series of dramatic demonstrations for your kid. It will take courage and ingenuity on your part; it may be fun as well. Here's how to do it.

First, pick some minor situation that bothers you. It need not be anything your kid does, although it might be. Let it be a small thing that happens fairly often, such as:

Somebody always leaves the toothpaste out on the sink instead of putting it away in the drawer.

The kids get into noisy arguments when we're all at the supper table.

Things keep getting left on the stairway, where I'm afraid I'll trip on them going up and down.

Second, use all your imagination to think of something you could do if this were to happen again that would meet the following conditions:

a. It would make you feel better to do it; it would ease your zing.

b. It would hurt no one, nor would it be aimed directly at your kid.

c. It could be a little zany—unreasonable, outrageous, unexpected, or startling.

d. It would be dramatic enough that others, especially your kid, would be sure to notice it.

e. It would have some relationship to the incident which bothers you, without blaming anyone else for it or giving anyone negative attention.

f. It is something you have full power to accomplish yourself.

Some things you might decide to do, for example, for the incidents we've mentioned:

Write a large notice on the bathroom mirror—in toothpaste—that you want the toothpaste put away.

Pick up your dinner, ceremoniously arrange it on a tray, carry it into your bedroom and shut the door, and eat it alone and in peace and quiet.

Take anything you find on the stairway and throw it under the house, or on the roof, or into the bathtub. (This would not be directed at "your kid's clothes" but at "any clothes on the stairway.")

We'll talk more about the kinds of things you can do after it's clear what to do with them.

When you've thought of something like this that you would be willing to do, hold it in mind, and then:

Third, announce to your family what you want as far as this item goes—in a mild, relaxed I-statement, with no you's.

I'd like the toothpaste kept in the drawer.

I really want peace and a friendly atmosphere at the supper table.

I want the stairway clear of things.

This is a kind of mini-establishing what you think is fair.

Fourth, wait until the situation comes up again (you can be reasonably sure that it will.)

Fifth, repeat to your family what you want in this situation, and this time *tell them what you will do if you don't get what you want.*

I really want the toothpaste kept in the drawer. If that doesn't happen, I'll write on the mirror in toothpaste.

I really want peace and quiet at the table. If I don't get it, I'll take my dinner into the bedroom and eat by myself.

I want the stairway clear. If I find it cluttered, I'll throw the things in the bathtub.

At this point, you may be saying to yourself, "It isn't logical to spread toothpaste on the mirror if I want the bathroom clean and neat." True, it isn't logical, from the rather narrow perspective of the cleanliness of the bathroom. But your goal is much broader than the cleanliness of your bathroom, and from that broad perspective, other, narrower views of logic could well be quite illogical. Don't be trapped by logic, consistency, and so on. The toothpaste is a vehicle toward establishing your credibility.

Sixth, wait until the situation arises again (and after your last statement it is almost sure to come), and when it does—do what you said you would do. Do it with enjoyment.

And *seventh,* consider this step a success if you begin to experience a sense of exhilaration and even power as you do these things. We're aiming toward a feeling of *freedom* (you are not trapped by your kid or the situation), of *competence* (you can do things to take care of yourself), and of *exhilaration* (it's appropriate to feel joyous and expansive about all that you are free and able to do.)

Now, what kinds of things can you pick to do?

Choose something that you can do *in order to make yourself feel better.* Do not do it in order to teach your kid a lesson, nor to get even, nor to push him or her into doing anything. Pick something you can do for yourself and then forget.

Make sure that what you decide to do is directed at things rather than at people, and that when it comes time to do it, you act firmly and surely, without hesitation. In this step we're asking you to take physical action, and physical action can have either of two very different effects on the other people in your life, depending on how it's done. If you take action in an angry or upset, impulsive way, or if you direct it at another person or his or her belongings, it can excite others to retaliate and take action or even become violent against *you.* On the other hand, if you perform your action with a sure, firm, deliberate feeling, so that it's clearly something you're doing on purpose and feel you have a right to do, and if it does not invade another's person or property, it can inspire others, too, to behave more responsibly. That's one reason why we ask you never to attack your kid physically, and if you do decide to take action involving his or her possessions, to make a clear statement ahead of time that you mean to do so, and be sure it seems fair to you. If you do things this way you're unlikely to precipitate violence.

Make sure that each thing you decide to do is a specific and one-time action, and not a long term, repeated activity. We've seen parents get into drawn out contests by saying something like, "If you won't do the yard, I won't do the laundry." The kid responds with, "If you won't do the laundry, I won't do the yard," and the situation becomes a contest. Neither laundry nor yard gets done for a long time and your resentment builds. Make your thing something you do once, and that's the end of the incident.

That way, if the annoying problem comes up again, you're free to handle it in some new way, and meanwhile you're eased of your zing and can go about your life.

If the yard isn't done by four, I'll feel embarrassed to have anyone see me, and I'll wear a mask when the company comes over tonight.

Make each thing as zany and dramatic as you can be comfortable with. We can't tell you just how far to go in this direction because what's zany and dramatic depends so much on what the atmosphere has been in your family and what your particular style has been. In a family that is generally soft-spoken, polite, and reserved, some very small, only mildly dramatic things may have a large impact. In a different family, say one in which four or five kids have taken over and are openly running a single parent, it may take much more dramatic behavior to attract attention. For example:

Mrs. I. had always been very quiet and deferential. It was a dramatic event for her family when, in front of them all, she announced that she would take an extra pat of butter for her baked potato, and did so.

Mrs. B. told her family she was going to run away for three days. Then she packed a suitcase and did it.

In general, we think that the kind of parent who would read this book can't lose by being as zany and dramatic as possible. It's likely that a problem in the past has been that you've leaned too far in the dutiful, conventional direction and let your kid do all the unpredictable behaving. Consider, then, doing some things you've never done before and enjoying the feeling of daring that it can give you.

And finally, don't worry too much about getting the things you choose exactly right. It's better to do some and have them backfire a little than to hold off and continue to feel walked on.

Here are some things that desperate parents we have counselled have come up with or that we have suggested for them. Some of these break the rules we've just set up, and no doubt that reduced their effectiveness some, and yet—doing them at all can be a great improvement over what has been going on.

Quiet Mr. D. felt nearly overwhelmed because his very boisterous stepchildren openly ignored or insulted and were contemptuous of him. When we suggested he do something dramatic to demonstrate to them that he was there and would do whatever he said he would, he recalled that he had bought them the TV set they were using, and that it was kept in an upstairs room. In fact, the noise from this TV and the fact that the kids listened to it and ignored him was one of his complaints. He decided that the next time the kids ignored or insulted him, he could easily pick up the TV, take it to the window, and throw it out into the yard.

"I want to feel that I'm treated like a person around here. If I get the feeling I'm not, I'll throw the TV out the window."

A sensitive and vital woman, Mrs. W., told her family she was heartily dissatisfied with being awakened nearly every night by someone's entering the house around two or three A.M., and that the next time she was so awakened she would scream. A few days later her son, Matthew (16), once again came in very late. She got out of bed, put on a robe, walked out into the middle of the street, and screamed three times at the top of her voice, "Matthew W. is not fair!" Then she returned to the house and went to bed.

Mrs. T. had told everyone in the family how she felt a-bout the garbage job—that she wanted it done, and that she felt it was unfair for her to do it when she had so many other tasks for the family. We suggested that the next time she noticed the unemptied garbage bag, she say, "If the garbage isn't emptied by this afternoon, I'll serve it up for dinner." Then she was to get out the best silver and dishes, and very artistically serve the family bowls of sloppy coffee grounds, orange and potato peels, and so on.

Mrs. G. decided, in a session one of us had with her and

Mr. G., to say, "I get so upset when the laundry is just thrown on the floor instead of being put in the hamper, that I think the next time I find it I'll throw it off the balcony into the front yard." Her husband's clothes were included in the total that had been appearing on the floor. He responded, "Fair enough."

Mr. M. wanted to get more exercise into his daily life and decided to use this approach to a problem he had been having. He told his kids, "I have trouble driving the car when there's fighting and shouting going on. If it happens again, I will get out and walk."

When you've done several things like this, you may sense that your kid is beginning to see you in a slightly different way. You may catch a puzzled or thoughtful expression when your kid looks at you, or he or she may begin to consult you, asking you whether you'll be home or whether you'll be making dinner, or do an occasional considerate thing for you, like asking whether you'd like some of the munchies he's fixing for himself. Even more important, you will find that you are becoming more confident and comfortable doing active things to take care of yourself. You'll begin to notice that when a problematic situation comes up and you feel a zing, your first thought is, "What can I do to make this better for me?" rather than, "My kid is misbehaving." Hope may come to you, too, a surge of joyous feeling that says, "I do not have to put up with unfair treatment! I can always take care of myself!"

Now begin gradually to extend this same approach to other, somewhat more important things that have bothered you, ultimately including the parent's-life items that are still a problem for you.

Here are a few examples of how parents can use the Step Four approach to work on these parent's-life items if previous steps do not resolve them:

Andy, I really want freedom from the dog messes left lying around so long. I will not tolerate them any further. If I see any more of them, I will find another home for the dog.

Sandy, I feel bad about having people in my house when I don't know about it. If I get any feeling at all that it's happening again, I'll arrange to have someone house sit for a week.

Bill, if I don't get the money for the long distance calls to Ann Arbor by Tuesday, I will begin disconnecting the hand-piece and carrying it in my purse.

(Note: On the newer models of the conventional style phones, the hand-piece can be disconnected or re-connected in about two seconds and the phone will still ring if a small object is placed in the cradle where the hand-piece normally goes.)

Carol, I want to feel secure about my things. If I miss any more of my money or clothes, I will definitely call the police and ask them to investigate.

The four steps you have just completed comprise our basic recommendations for dealing with the parent's-life items on your list. If you've worked through this whole book thus far, and then actually followed through on several items using the Step Four approach, we think you will find that you are no longer feeling nearly so helpless about problems as you once did, that instead you are feeling more and more able to take care of yourself when they come up. By this time you'll be coming through to your son or daughter not only as someone who deeply respects your kid's rights, but as a more definite person yourself, someone more to be respected than before. For the great majority of readers of this book, the problems you've been having with your kid will have changed for the better. The task from now on is one of maintaining this improvement and continuing to practice the things you have learned.

For a few parents in unusually difficult situations, we will describe a further step to be taken—a parental strike. We advise that you go on with this step only if you have sincerely worked through everything else in the book, and then only if the problems you experience with your kid

are serious and quite painful to you. This step can sometimes help when all else has failed, and we certainly think
you should take it rather than continuing in a situation that
is demeaning or painful to you. However, we don't recommend using it if other approaches seem to be helping, or
if you have only minor problems left. In that case, it would
be better to practice more thoroughly the skills you have
already covered, or, perhaps, leave things as they are for
a time to see how they settle out.

> Mrs. T. was feeling unbearably pressured by the things
> her daughter, Natalie (16) was doing, and she asked for
> help in finding a foster home for her. We asked her to
> come for counselling instead, and she agreed. Natalie her-
> self refused regular counselling meetings, but her mother
> came and worked hard at the kinds of things we talk about
> in this book. After a few months almost all of the problems
> she had experienced were gone, and she was living on good
> terms with her daughter. She actually enjoyed warm talks
> with her and a feeling that she and Natalie cared about each
> other. Two things continued to bother her: Natalie clearly
> was going on with an active sexual life (which shocked and
> worried her mother), and she continued to strew her clothes
> all over the hallway (which merely annoyed her mother).
> Mrs. T. decided not to push for further changes but to
> rest content with the progress both she and Natalie had
> made. She decided to take care of herself as far as Nat-
> alie's sex life went by furnishing Natalie with birth control
> pills in order to assuage her (the mother's) anxiety about
> possible pregnancy. She also decided to imagine that she
> had a pet bear who naturally strewed things about, but was
> worth keeping anyway. She took care of herself by putting
> a large cardboard box in the closet at the end of the hall
> and scooping all the clothes into it when she came home
> at the end of her working day.

For this parent, it would not have been appropriate
to go on to Step Five. She had few problems left, and it
seemed likely she could handle those by working further
on what we've already covered in this book. For some other
parents, however, this step may be the only thing definite
enough to make a difference. It seems appropriate for sit-

uations in which, for example, a kid is running the family like a dictator, or is doing adult things (like having sex, or even babies, or driving cars) without taking responsibility for them, or has parked on the family as a dead weight and refuses to do anything to care for him or herself. Kids are just people, and like everyone else, they, too, can become dictators, tyrants, manipulators, if the situation allows for it. In such cases strong measures like a parental strike may be needed to get everyone back onto a saner level.

Carolyn (16) ignored her parents most of the time; when she did condescend to speak to them it was usually to express contempt or to give them orders. She was already feeling entirely free on kid's-life items, and she simply ignored her parents' attempts to stand up for themselves on parent's-life items. She seemed so deeply convinced that they had no rights that a strike may have been the only way they could show her otherwise.

Carl (15) had got his fifteen-year old girl friend pregnant and then informed his family that he was moving her in to live with them. His parents objected, saying, among other things, that they did not like the idea of the two minors having sex in their son's bedroom. Carl responded to all their objections with tantrums and dire threats to kill himself if he did not get his way. He did concede, though, that he and his girlfriend would not occupy the same bedroom; she, he said, would take over his mother's sewing room. He proceeded to move her and many bags and boxes in the next day. An hour or so later the two kids went to Carl's mother to ask her what dinner was going to be.

These parents had so little successful experience in standing up for themselves, and the situation was developing so fast, that we felt a build-up of assertive techniques would not be enough. We recommended an immediate and firm parental strike, in which it would be made clear to Carl that he could choose to live as an adult with his girlfriend only if he took responsibility for it, and that living as a child-couple in his parents' home was not one of his choices.

Barbara (15) refused to go to school and instead invited

rather tough friends in to party with her while her mother was at work. Her mother told her what she wanted, made agreements with her, went to bat with school and other officials to get Barbara what she said she wanted. Barbara always cooperated in working out agreements, and promised to abide by them, but then went on in her disturbing ways exactly as before. We agreed with the school counselor that it was appropriate for Barbara's mother to strike.

We ask you to think your situation over and decide what direction is right for you to take now. If things have improved through your work in this book, you are doing something very right, and the job is to learn to do it even more thoroughly. On the other hand, if parent's-life items are still a major problem for you, and a strike seems fair, then go ahead with Step Five feeling definite and confident about it!

Step Five

Up to now, everything we've suggested for you to do presupposes that you are going to continue your part in a conventional parent-kid relationship—that is, that you will live with your kid and provide him or her not only with material things—a home, food, clothes, medical care, perhaps allowance, and so on—but also with more intangible forms of parental support. However, if it's to be fair, the parent-kid relationship, like any other, should be a two-way street. The parent should experience rewards for providing care and support, and the rewards—knowing the kid is developing well, a reasonably good relationship, a feeling of loving and being loved—ought to be great enough that the parent enjoys the supporting. If you're not getting the rewards, then we think you're being disloyal to yourself: you're making yourself give without reasonable return. Your kid, too, is probably not benefitting fully from the relationship. We think that a kid who steadfastly refuses to join in a cooperative relationship with the parents has some important learning to do and may be best able to do it through living without some or all of the parental support you have been giving.

If this relationship were with any other person we can think of—a friend, a boss or employee, a neighbor, a spouse—and you were still feeling unfairly treated after so much hard work, you might well have considered pulling back from it somehow or completely withdrawing. We see no valid reason why this relationship should be treated any differently, especially since your kid's becoming independent some day is an inherent aim in this particular relationship from the beginning. In fact, looking at this as simply a relationship between two human beings *both of whom are free to leave it if they wish* may be the best thing for it. Therefore our basic recommendation for Step Five is that you *announce your intention of withdrawing from the conventional parent-kid relationship in some way unless something happens to make you happier in it. Then carry this through.*

We realize that for some parents, this is not at all simple, even when kids are far overstepping reasonable boundaries. You may be one of these parents; you may have compelling reasons for wanting to keep a traditional parent-child relationship going with your teenager in spite of all the trouble you're experiencing. One of those reasons may be the attitude of our society right now. Nowadays if a spouse treats you as your kid has been doing, society—by which we mean your relatives, friends, and the legal establishment—will generally support you in getting a divorce. However, that same society may go to extra lengths to persuade you that you should and must continue to be responsible for your kid and put up with the mistreatment no matter how bad it is. Unless you are rich enough to pay for private schools or other institutions, or poor enough to receive state aid, you're likely to have a much harder time withdrawing from this relationship than from any other we know of.

This attitude of society can be a real pressure upon you; it can make you afraid to behave as your common sense tells you is right. Both you and your kid are aware of this attitude, and we think that's one of the factors that helps *create* the parent-kid relationship as a one-way street. In other words, *both you and your kid may believe that you are not free to leave the relationship,* and because of this belief you may be putting up with more and your kid may be dishing out more than would otherwise be the case.

Taking Step Five may make for an improved relationship between you and your kid, or it may not. Be prepared to have it turn out either way, and to feel good about carrying it through in any case. In our opinion, it's better to feel free to take Step Five, no matter how it turns out, than to continue to feel trapped in a situation that's making you feel unhappy.

Begin this step with one or two partial strikes.

Think over the parental support things you do "for" your kid—things into which you would not put so much life energy if it were not for him or her. For you, these may be things like the following:

Talking with him or her—feeling concerned, interested, affectionate.
Making supper every night.
Buying groceries for two (or four, or six).
Sending out the payment for the orthodontist.
Teaching him or her to drive.
Allowing him or her to have a key to the house.
Giving him or her an allowance, lunch money, money for clothes.
Doing laundry.
Coming home every night whether you want to or not.
Making a special room available in the house for this person.
Providing a place to live in—a house or apartment.

Now decide that from now on, you will do *only what you want to* of these things.

The next time you find yourself about to do one or another of these things, ask yourself whether you feel like doing it. If you do, go ahead and do it. If not, say:

I'm going to skip making supper tonight. (Or—I'm not going to buy groceries this week.) It makes me feel I give and don't get anything back.

I'll not be taking you to practice driving tomorrow. I feel I've been doing more than my share, and I'm not going to keep giving unless things get more fair around here.

I'm not going to do your laundry this week. I feel put upon when I give and don't see any return. I'm not going to do that to myself.

Then go about your business. If your kid does something— such as doing his or her task, or being pleasant to you, or whatever—that makes you feel like doing the thing after all, then say:

I'm feeling good about doing this after all.

If your kid does not do this, keep your word. Abstain from these things you have been doing "for" your kid unless you really feel like doing them.

Sometimes parents hesitate to "strike" in this way because they're taking care of *several* people, and they feel they can't stop doing things for one without depriving the others, too. Please do not decide you must put up with unfair treatment because of this. Use your head to figure out a way of striking that you feel *would* be fair to the others, if you easily can. If you can't, then we recommend that you strike anyway. This may inconvenience the others in the family (it may also motivate them to take some responsibility for helping you resolve this kid problem!)— but we think that is better than being disloyal to your inner self by giving up on taking care of it.

Here are a few examples of how parents can make a partial strike by withholding something they have been providing.

Andy (15) and his parents seemed to be in a contest over

when he was to come in at night. The parents wanted the house closed down at midnight. Andy regularly missed this time by anywhere from five minutes to many hours, and his mother regularly spent sleepless nights because she couldn't relax until she knew things were tamped down. At last she decided to take care of herself by getting out of the contest. She couldn't quite bring herself to leave Andy to shift for himself, but she said, "This house is definitely closed after midnight. If you're not in at that time, I'll put your sleeping bag out on the porch, and expect not to be disturbed until morning."

Every time Linda (14) ran away, her parents worried about her welfare and felt painfully uncertain about whether she would return. They tried to find their daughter, and urged her, through her friends, to come home. However, her father began to feel resentful at going through this ordeal so often, and realized he felt it was unfair to him and Linda's mother. He told his daughter, "Linda, it is a real hassle to me every time you run away. Next time it happens I want a complete vacation from you and from the hassle for three days. I want you to stay out of the house for at least that long."

For several months Pete's parents had done everything they could think of to "help" Pete (15), who had taken to cutting and failing school, coming in very late at night, bringing strangers into the house while his parents were at work, and so on. He snubbed and ignored his parents and would not contribute to family life in any way. His parents asked what was troubling him; they took him to counselors and went to school conferences to help work out plans he might like. Nothing they did seemed to make any difference. At last the father became disgusted. He decided he wanted to continue supporting Pete as far as furnishing home and groceries, but that he would no longer invest himself—his interest and attention—without any return. Therefore he stopped talking to Pete—at all. The boy was very surprised at this, and made the first positive changes anyone had seen—in order to get back on speaking terms with his father.

Tony's mother was nearly wild with worry about his activities, which included violent behavior at home (breaking furniture if he did not like what his parents said), using and probably dealing drugs from the house, loud stereo at all hours, and nightly absences of many hours. At one point she began to wonder why she was putting so much of her life into the situation when Tony (16) showed no signs of wanting or appreciating her. She told him, "Tony, I've provided a room for you for a long time, but at the same time I've always wanted a sewing room for myself. I want some signs that you want me to be your mother, and if I don't get them I'll stop supplying the room for you. I'll make it into a sewing room for myself.

In these partial strikes you're making the clearest possible announcement that you want a change. If you are doing the things we have described so far in this book, you've been outstandingly fair, persistent, and respecting of your kid's rights in leading up to it. If you do not get a favorable response to this plea, it's time for a more total strike, one which involves some separation from your kid.

The first move in this strike is the hardest: it is to *decide what kind of separation you can and would be willing to bring about.* It's hard because the idea of "throwing my kid out" can have the sound of abandoning a helpless waif to misfortune, and none of us is willing to do that. Nonetheless, seeing our kids as helpless waifs is one of the habits that has brought about so much trouble in the first place, so we recommend you change to a different picture of what you will be doing. Ask yourself seriously, "How would I act if my kid, behaving just as he or she is, were an equal age adult in my home?" "How would I act if my kid were nineteen?" Then act accordingly; treat your kid as you would treat an adult.

There are several kinds of separation you could go for.

You could arrange for your kid to live with a relative.

Mr. and Mrs. A's son (16) was running wild. The parents told him that spending the summer at his uncle's ranch, working for his keep, was a possibility for him, and that unless they felt better about him within a week, that was the only possibility they were providing; living at home would not be one of his options.

Legally, in most states a parent can provide for the support of a minor child in any suitable way of the parent's choosing. You do not have to provide that support under the same roof with you.

You could send your kid to a boarding school.

If you can afford it and your kid wants to do this, it could be a satisfactory solution for you. If your kid doesn't want this, the situation may be different. Legally you are on firm ground since you have the authority to decide such things for your minor child. However, boarding schools will often refuse to enroll unwilling students.

You could give your kid permission to go live with another family, in another household.

Eric (16) thought his friend's parents were "super-neat" and his friend's older sister had grown up and left home, leaving a spare bedroom. Eric negotiated with his friend's mother to be able to live with them and pay $15 a week room and board from his after-school job. Eric's parents agreed. (Within four months Eric wanted to come home and his parents agreed. He was a different kid!)

Kids frequently know of families who would be willing to have them stay with them, either with or without your financial contribution. You might even know of a family with a problem similar to yours that would be willing to trade kids.

This kind of resolution, in which your kid lives with another family not related to yours, has a very important advantage. It is immediately obvious to the kid that he or she must make that family actively want to continue having him or her live with them. Almost certainly your kid knows how to make the family want to continue with the arrangement and the actual doing of it is excellent practice for adult living.

You could separate from your kid but continue to give some financial support.

Marcia (16) had a boyfriend and a circle of friends outside the family, and did little with her mother except fight. Her mother was unhappy in this situation, and Marcia was hostile about having to be home at all. They talked it over, and Marcia's mother decided to furnish Marcia with $100 a month until she reached eighteen, and to allow her to make her own arrangements about where to live.

You could declare to the juvenile authorities that your kid is out of your parental control, that you want him or her made a ward of the court, and that you will not continue living with your kid.

Juvenile authorites (and police) may try to get you to change your mind and may even tell you that what you are proposing cannot be done. Generally, though, it can. Your kid will probably be placed in a temporary juvenile facility and you will no doubt be charged for the support. However, the closer your kid is getting to eighteen, the less enthusiastic the authorities will be about doing anything like this.

You could pure-and-simply put your kid out.

If your kid is legally an adult either because of age (eighteen in most states) or being emancipated (e.g. by being married or having a child) then this possibility is perfectly within your legal right. If your kid is a minor, then taking this action would not be legal and we would not recommend it, any more than we would recommend your going 60 in a 55 mph zone. If you decide to take this kind of action bear in mind that it is not legal and that as a result there may be consequences to you. You may decide that the risk is worth it to you. We have noticed that many people in this country who are under eighteen go on their own every year—some by their own choice, some because they've been "thrown out" by their parents. We tend not to hear about them because they go one by one without the publicity of high school graduation and so on, but there's a whole segment of society that lives in this way. Some of them return home after a time; others go on to make their way on their own. Many become successful business and family persons.

> Perry (16) spent most of his time running with a rather tough group inclined to petty lawbreaking. He would neither go to school, get a job, nor help around the house. He used the home only as a sort of convenient pad, coming in and out as he wished and incidentally littering the place with pornographic literature and objects like torn-apart wallets that had the look of being stolen property. His parents' attempts to get a better deal had no apparent effect. At last, when Perry phoned home after an absence of several days, his father told him to stay out.

After you've decided what you are willing to do, confront your kid once again, this time with a statement that has two important parts.

In the first part tell him or her *what you want*.

In the second part tell your kid exactly *what you will do* if you do not get what you want *by a certain time*.

Alice, I want an equal relationship with you in which each of us makes a contribution. As I see it, your part is to get yourself educated or else contribute room and board, and to help out here at home. If I don't feel you're doing your part by a week from now, I will no longer live with you.

Ben, I'm still unhappy living with you. I want help with keeping the place reasonably neat, and a more pleasant atmosphere. If after two weeks I still don't feel I'm getting it, I will set it up so you can live with your uncle, if you like. In any case I will no longer provide for you here.

Carol, I'm simply not happy living with you this way. If things aren't better within a few days, I say: I won't play any more; the deal's off. I'm willing to contribute some to your support wherever you're living, until you're eighteen, and I will want you out of the house.

Once you've made this announcement, meaning it, wait until the end of the time you have set. If the situation with your kid improves enough to satisfy you by that time, fine. You've accomplished a change and the only job now is to continue to stand up for yourself. If the situation has not improved by that time, *do* whatever you said you would do. Do it without dramatics, guilt, hesitation, or doubt.

Mrs. S. told her son (16) that unless she felt a major improvement in the situation, she wanted him out by the end of June. On the first day of July, having seen no change, she packed all of his things in cardboard cartons and set them outside, locked the house, and went about her business. (Her son picked up his things, moved in with friends several years older, got a job as a mechanic, and became self-supporting. No one knows why he never did this while at home, but an improvement in the situation was felt by all concerned.)

Kay (17) held open house in her bedroom for her boyfriend, by whom she was pregnant. He came in and out and spent the night as he pleased, even though Kay's mother, Mrs. L., said, "If this happens one more time, I want you both moved out of my house." He did come in again without permission, and when Mrs. L. said, "I want you both out," the boyfriend shoved her. Mrs. L. called the police. When they came, she agreed not to charge the boyfriend with assault for the shoving if the two young people would leave. The police supervised their move to a friend's apartment.

Having your kid out of the house is probably *not* the end of the story. Your strike has more moves.

The first one is to *hold a positive state of mind in the period immediately after the separation.* Hopefully, when you took action to get your kid out you were seeing him or her as a person able to care for him or herself, and you felt matter-of-fact and good about your right to be treated fairly. Maintain these attitudes against the pressures which may assail you now. A load of guilt can come down upon parents who have stood up for themselves as you have, especially if they are women, and kids and society in general often play powerfully upon that guilt to persuade you to change your mind. Be prepared to hold firm and feel relaxed even against:

Phone calls from neighbors or perhaps from parents of the family your kid is staying with, telling you how wonderful your kid is and how you too could be a great parent if you would only do so and so. (They won't use exactly these words but you will get the idea.)

Phone calls from friends of your kid who ask to speak with him or her as if they did not know the situation, and then begin pressuring you to change your mind, telling you how wonderful, scared, loving, disturbed, etc., your kid is.

Pressure from *your* parents or other relatives who say, "You can't do this to your kid..." "What will happen to him or her?"
(If this happens, you might tell these relatives that it would be all right with you if they would like your kid to live with them.)

Phone calls from police.
(As in the case of calls from neighbors and other "concerned" outsiders, the police at this point will probably have heard only your kid's story. Since you will have gone through all of the earlier steps in this book by now, and will not have taken this Step Five action for anything trivial, your side of the story will very probably induce understanding and perhaps even help from the police.)

The other, and last, important part of your strike is to *be true to yourself when, as almost always happens, you and your kid get in touch again.* A few days or a few weeks after separating, you're likely to be talking together again, either because your kid calls you, or because you make the first move and contact him or her. When that happens, it's possible that you may learn that your son or daughter is well satisfied with being out and, in his or her own eyes, is doing fine. If this happens, hold in mind what you're after, and if it is a happy, relaxed long term relationship, be friendly and treat your kid as you would any other dear, adult, and independent friend. It's more likely that your kid will turn out to be not so satisfied with being out, and will ask for financial help or ask you to take him or her back into the house. If this happens, remember to *consult your inner being* to decide how you feel about it. If that inner being feels good about it, consider giving the financial help requested. If that inner being feels comfortably sure things can really be better, then consider living with the kid again. Tell him or her that you definitely want to be treated fairly, and that as long as you feel you are, he or she is welcome to return. If your inner being tells you nothing has changed and you'll be expected to do all the giving again, say, "No." It's not too different from a situation in which you and a spouse have separated for some reason. Once that separation has occurred, you have the right to stay apart or go back together as it *feels right to you.*

Ten

A Look Ahead

You've now read through, and perhaps worked through, a whole book's worth of ideas for relating to your kid in a different way. What can you reasonably look forward to after taking the trouble to learn and to follow this program? How is your kid likely to respond to all this?

In everything we've recommended we've assumed that you would like a positive relationship with your kid say ten years from now. That is very likely to happen if you've done what we have suggested in this book—even if you've gone all the way, through Chapter 9, Step Five!

Parents sometimes undertake the things we suggest with trepidation. They're afraid that if they drop their controls over kid's-life items their kids will run wild, or feel unloved, or become alienated from their parents. They're afraid that if they stand up for themselves on parent's-life items the kids will be angry, or feel deprived, or reject them. These are parents' fears. However, what actually happens when they go ahead with this program is almost always the reverse of these fears. Kids become less wild and more responsible; they know they are cared for and they feel closer to their parents. Rather than feeling angry, deprived, or rejecting, they tend eventually to feel respecting toward their parents.

The immediate results of using this approach are often a brief resistance and then very quick improvement in the parent-kid relationship. When you begin to stand up for yourself, for example, your kid may sulk, or agitate, may make scenes, may even walk out on you. This lasts *until the kid becomes convinced that you mean it and that he or she cannot make you give in.* At that point you may unexpectedly get smiles and a relaxed and happy demeanor as the kid begins to cooperate in ways he or she knows are right. This cheerful, cooperative behavior tends to last until something once again suggests that you are caving in and will put up with unfair treatment. It's almost as if the kid *wants* the limit you set and feels happy and satisfied at getting it. We've seen this happen time and again.

> Tom (16), doing some carpentry work for his weekly house contribution, was making the place ring with four-letter words as he missed nails and had to pull them out. His father said, "Tom, I want freedom from four letter words around here." Tom responded with a muttered curse. His father said, "I realize you're mad—and I do want freedom from four letter words." At this, Tom slammed his hammer down and left the house, apparently in a fury. Fifteen minutes later he returned, took up his hammer, and was soon heard whistling happily as he worked, with no sign of resentment.

> Andy's mother was much disturbed by Andy's late nights, but she dreaded doing anything about it. She had told Andy (15) many times that she wanted the house closed down by midnight; he had completely ignored these statements. She was afraid that if she went any further he would feel angry, or rejected, there would be a scene, she would feel like a bad mother, and so on. Finally, though, she geared herself up to say, "Andy, this house is definitely closed at midnight. If you're not in it by then, I'll put your sleeping bag out on the porch." Then came the response she had been so dreading: Andy thought for a moment, and then he said, "OK, Mom. That's fair."

The longer term results of going ahead with this program are an improved relationship between two independent people, the parent and the kid, and often more closeness than before.

> After years of having a very hard time living with their son, Michael's parents finally, when he reached eighteen, threw him out. Michael left the house, but after three weeks he came back and asked if he could live at home while he was going to school. His parents said, "The rules are still the same, and everyone who lives here has to follow them." Michael agreed to this, moved back in, and from then on, as if by magic, was very pleasant to live with! He and his parents became closer than they had ever been. Apparently it took his eighteenth birthday to convince his parents that they had a right to stand up for themselves and mean it, and Michael responded well to finally getting this firmness from them.

> Steven's parents bewailed the fact that Steven (17) never wanted to go anywhere or do anything with them. However, as part of the program in this book, they stopped insisting that he do so, and began going on outings without him, simply inviting Steven to come if he wished but not pressing him at all. The fourth or fifth such outing without Steven was a weekend campout at the beach. As the rest of the family sat around the campfire Friday night, they were beautifully surprised to hear a car pull up and Steven and a friend get out and join them—because they *wanted* to come. The relaxed, pleasant, accepting way they all felt toward each other that evening was much nearer what the parents wanted than the strained ways they had felt when they forced Steven to come with them.

In some situations, particularly if parents have a hard time using this approach and must move into it very slowly, the results seem not so positive at first, and the relationship shows its improvement later. We think that even if you and your kid part company and live apart for many months, acting according to the philosophy in this book is likely to get you a positive relationship with your kid later on. The parent-kid relationship can be very intense—so intense that none of you may understand or be easy with it in the teen years. When the high charge of it dissipates a little and you can all get a better perspective on it, it's likely that you and your kid will make friends again. We've known many situations in which a man or woman of 20, 25, or older "comes home again" in the sense of meeting the parents anew and making peace with them. If you want that sort of thing to happen, stay open for the possibility; it's likely to come.

If you've stayed with us all this way and sincerely worked through this book, we think it's time for you to give yourself thanks and appreciation for having done and understood so much. We believe you have probably made a major turn-around in your way of relating with your kid. You may now have a strong, comfortable feeling that:

Upset and crisis between you and your kid presents an opportunity for *you* to grow and change.

You are an equal human being, with equal human rights.

Your kid is a competent and worthy person.

You are competent too, and there is no situation in which you are helpless; there is always something *you* can do to help yourself.

Your job is to fulfill, express, take care of your inner being.

You are responsible for what *you* do.

Your kid is responsible for what he or she does.

Having come this far, your task now is to maintain these attitudes. Basically, they come down to two principles:

Seeing your kid as a capable, worthy being.

Believing he or she is able, trustworthy, and responsible.

Communicating that belief to him or her by:
1. Saying directly, "I trust you to make the right decision for you."
2. Listening with respect—that is, while assuming that he or she can solve his or her own problems.
3. Enjoying your kid's decision making.

Feeling comfortable about standing up for fair treatment for yourself.

To agree with these in principle is easy; to learn to live them in all the different situations life presents you with is difficult. It's for that reason we suggest that you reread this book every few months or so as long as there is tension in the situation between you and your kid.

Appendix A

Questions Parents Ask

Isn't it my job to guide my kid? Doesn't he need my guidance?

Indeed, yes, we think your son does need your guidance. However, no matter what you do, your son is likely to notice and be influenced by it; in that sense you can't help but guide him. What is important is where your guidance points—whether it says to your son, "Follow my decisions because I know best and you can't make good decisions," or whether it says, "You can make your own good decisions."

To provide the best guidance, you must let go and trust your kid to run his or her own life. Don't throw out your ability to control things, though. Turn it back on yourself and use it to get into your own life everything you want.

Shouldn't my husband and I be consistent with each other?

We think consistency is very important, but not consistency of the sort that decrees you and your spouse must handle everything in the same way. The two of you are different people, with different wants and different feelings. Further, for both of you, those wants and feelings are constantly changing. So it usually doesn't work to require consistency in the sense that you both reach the same decisions about how to handle things.

There's another kind of consistency that's much more meaningful. Basically, it is being *consistent with yourself* in the sense of always being guided by your own feelings and wants, and knowing that no matter how the situation changes, you can count on yourself to take care of yourself. If you're consistent in this way, your wants and feelings may change, and your behavior will be changeable to fit them, but you'll be consistently true to yourself. Your doing this is important for both you and your kid.

Further, if you're loyal to yourself in this sense, and one of your deep wants is a happy relationship with your spouse, you'll be loyal to him in that you will want his ways of doing things to work well, and you will not sabotage them in any way. You'll trust your spouse to be able to handle problems that come up for him, in his own unique way.

Aren't parents supposed to set limits? How can I do that if I'm not even going to try to control what she does?

Yes, it does seem important to set limits. You can do so by setting limits, not on how your kid will behave, but on *how you will be treated.* You can communicate clearly what kind of treatment you want, make a firm stand to get it, and, finally, let it be known what you will do to take care of yourself if you do not get it.

Isn't my kid my responsibility? She didn't ask to be born.

We've heard both parents and kids make this "didn't ask to be born" or "didn't ask to be adopted" remark, usually to justify a one-way relationship in which the parent feels guilty and obligated and the kid feels resentful about not being given more. The remark sounds illogical to us; in the context in which it is used here, you didn't ask to be born either. We think of being born rather as a gift—and the essence of the gift is the right and obligation to be responsible for one's own self. What else does any human being have?

No, we think your kid is not your responsibility, because he or she is not your possession. Your kid is responsible for him or herself; you are responsible for yourself.

Isn't it selfish to take care of myself?

No. In the sense in which we describe it here, it's just the reverse.

Being unselfish and caring for others seems to us to

be the highest form of human living. There's something almost paradoxical about it, though. It seems to be meaningful only if you give to others *because you want to*—that is, if doing so is at the same time a taking care of yourself, so that you're giving because it makes you feel good to see the other person happy. If you give out of duty, because you should, or while grudging the giving, or expecting some return, the giving becomes something different.

We think that it's important to learn this kind of giving because-you-want-to, and that a first step in this direction is learning to take care of yourself. It is our experience that when persons become sensitive to and loyal to their own wants, they then find that one of the deepest of those wants is to help others, to love and live cooperatively with them. Then taking care of others turns out to be the deepest form of taking care of oneself.

This is a hard time in the world for kids to grow up in; I feel sorry for my daughter and want to help her.

We can certainly understand feeling sorry, but at the same time, it is a damaging point of view to take toward your daughter. She'd be better off if you let her know you believed she could make out in life just fine.

What about my kid's self image? I often tell her I love her so she'll know she's cared for.

We agree that a kid's self image and her feeling able to cope is very important. So the question is: What can you, the parent, do to improve that self esteem and your kid's feeling of being able to cope? The best thing we see that will help is your changing your picture of your daughter so that you see her as someone who is capable, and holding to that view, letting all of your actions be guided by it.

How can my changing help my son? Can I make any difference by myself if he won't try to change too?

Yes, you can do much by yourself.

Some of your son's misbehavior may be done in relation to whatever way you're behaving. If you change what you do, he will no longer be able to act in the same way, and from your point of view, his new behavior is likely to be an improvement.

Some of his misbehavior may stem straight and simply from the way he is, separate from you. You can learn to stop adding your useless worry to these ways of acting.

And certainly, you can learn to take responsibility for making your own life happy. That not only helps you, but it's probably the one most effective thing you can do to maximize the chances of your son's changing in a positive direction.

Do you mean just let them run wild and don't care about them?

It is one thing to say, in effect, "Go ahead and do whatever you want. I don't care." It is another to say, "I am worried that if you do such and so, you will suffer in some way because of it, and I have faith in your ability to do what is best for you. And I do care for your well being." It is, of course, the latter view that we are encouraging.

But what about being close? We used to be close, but he's pulled away.

When you were close, you were big, he was small. You said what was what and he generally did as you said. The teenage years are a preparation for a time when you will both be big and neither will say what is to be what for the other. Therefore he is pulling away from the "me small" role and getting ready for the "me big" time. This pulling away is natural and usually temporary. Be patient and the closeness is likely to return in a new, adult form.

What about the dangers? I'm afraid to let my kid do what he wants because he might get hurt.

We care deeply about the dangers—enough to say a sometimes painful truth: Your continuing to try to control your kid pushes him or her closer into danger. Your giving your kid responsibility for his or her own actions enables him or her to develop the best protection against danger: a clear-thinking intelligence that's geared to take care of itself.

What if my spouse won't cooperate with me in using this approach?

We have two important things to say here.

1. The principles we've described in this book apply not only to teenagers. They work in all sorts of other relationships as well. If the way your spouse relates with you and/or the kids is a problem for you, list those problems, divide them into spouse's-life and my-own-life items, and use all the principles in this book to work them out.

2. Be sure to "let" your spouse and your kid have their own relationship in whatever way seems best to them. For example, if you want to get along with your kid in a relaxed and affectionate way and are doing it, and your spouse and your kid seem to relate to each other through orders, resentments, recriminations—let them. Stick to taking care of problems that impinge on your life and the way in which you relate to others.

Even if your spouse is cooperating but not doing it "right" as you are, don't be the enforcer, but let your spouse do things the way it suits him or her.

Don't parents have any rights?

How could you ever doubt it?

Of course you have rights—and it's your job to champion them!

Appendix B

Some Parents and How They Coped

A Parent Who Coped Twice

Even parents who have a very hard time dropping controls over their kids' lives can eventually become comfortable doing so and benefit from it. For Mrs. F., this took diligent and persistent work, but her eventual success was worth it.

She had been widowed when her two children were quite young, and was supporting the family and her invalid father on her survivor's benefits (her husband had been a Navy officer). Things had gone well until Carl, the younger child, was 14 and in the middle of the ninth grade. Until then he had generally been obedient to his mother and was no problem either at school or at home. For example, although he preferred to go out to play after school, he grumblingly but obediently did his homework first. Then things changed. He began refusing to do his homework until after dinner, then occasionally not at all. Over a period of a few months his school performance went from satisfactory to poor, with some discipline problems and extensive truancy as well. In addition, he began to spend time with another boy with whom he started getting into mischief in the neighborhood.

Mrs. F., a very gentle person, very early in Carl's "problem" time found herself quite helpless to make any difference in his behavior, despite scoldings, pleadings, tears, appeals to honor the memory of his father, and so on. Both Mrs. F. and Carl seemed to believe that if he did well in school and generally behaved himself he was doing it for her rather than for himself.

After a particularly trying session with Carl's teacher, whom Carl had sassed, Mrs. F. called asking for counseling help, and we began working with her and Carl. Soon, however, Carl began "forgetting" to come to our meetings, and finally said he would not come at all. We did as we usually do when this happens—continued to work with Mrs. F. Like many of the parents we work with, Mrs. F. had much difficulty at first in giving up the idea that she should be able to control Carl's activities. Gradually, however, the reality of her powerlessness convinced her to begin trying something different, and she slowly and tentatively began applying the approach we describe in this book. Then one early July day, things seemed to take a turn for the worse. (They often do, as described in Chapter 4.) Carl and a friend were picked up by the police and put in Juvenile Hall for throwing lighted firecrackers into passing automobiles. By this time Mrs. F. had decided to let the full impact of the Juvenile Justice system be felt by Carl, trusting that he could cope with it. As a consequence, he had a stay at Juvenile Hall, and when he came out he was on probation.

During the rest of the summer and into fall, Mrs. F. slowly but steadily moved to let Carl's decisions be his own. During this same time Carl slowly but just as steadily began to become more responsible. Although he was still acting up some as he started his sophomore year, the problems steadily diminished until by the spring semester he was no longer failing in anything, was not getting into trouble in school or elsewhere, and he and his mother were on excellent, loving terms.

Happy ending of the story—right? Wrong.

At about this time Carl's older sister, who was then just turning 17, began to show some different behavior. Up to this time she had been no trouble at all to her mother, had done well in school, treated her invalid grandfather well—in short, the kind of kid any parent would find comfortable to be with. Then Sally made some startling changes, at least from her mother's point of view. She began cutting school. In the past she had been interested in boys, but they were always the "nice" boys, ones that her mother approved of, and she wasn't heavily involved with them. Now, she became very much interested in a boy several years older than her who lived down the street and who would come home roaring drunk in his pick-up. She became involved with him sexually, in such a flagrant way that her mother was bound to find out. One day, when her mother was gone but her grandfather was home in his bedroom right next to hers, she brought the boy in to her bedroom for a noisy, graphically sexual session that she certainly knew her grandfather would report to Mrs. F.

At this point, Mrs. F. again came for counseling, on this new problem, and Sally also agreed to come in. The two of them had always been quite close and affectionate, and they reaffirmed their feelings of affection for each other, and Sally said that she would give up this boyfriend. However, very shortly thereafter, she stopped coming to the counselling sessions and began seeing the same boy surreptitiously. Mrs. F. was distraught. Despite the fact that she had gone through the same kind of thing with Carl and had finally come to feel contented about dropping her controls over him, she was still caught in the helpless struggle to control Sally. It was almost as though she were starting over. But again, diligently and persistently, she worked at learning to drop her controlling habits. In the meantime, Sally did give up that boy friend but instead picked up another one who was 21 years old and was, in fact, put in a minimum security jail shortly after Sally met him. In this almost-prison, he could receive phone calls at certain times, and Sally spent long periods talking with him on the phone, incurring substantial phone bills in the process.

We worked with Mrs. F. to turn over to Sally complete responsibility for her own life, including her love life. Mrs. F. concentrated on things like making sure she wasn't paying phone bills for her daughter's calls to the boy friend.

(In a bit of throw-back to her old, controlling ways, Mrs. F. was thinking of making Sally give up her job, ostensibly "so she could study more," but really so that she wouldn't be able to pay for the phone bills and the mother could then use her inability to pay for the calls as an excuse to insist on Sally's not calling the boy friend. Fortunately it was rather easy to convince Mrs. F. that this devious ploy probably wouldn't work.)

For Mrs. F., the second time was just about as difficult as the first time. As with the first time, though, she did eventually succeed and by the time her daughter was 18 and had graduated from high school the two of them were on very good terms, somewhat as they had been when Sally was younger, but without the adult-kid flavor of those times. Rather, it was more like two loving grown-ups relating to each other. At this point, Sally is continuing with her education at a local college, is living at home for the time being, no longer has "raunchy" boy friends, and Mrs. F. is quite satisfied with the way things have worked out. Sally gave up the "raunchy" boy friends quite spontaneously, and in fact one day casually remarked to her mother that, "I don't think he (the incarcerated one) is the right kind of guy for me."

A Wholehearted Effort

Mr. and Mrs. B. had what could have been a very troubled situation. We tell their story in some detail to illustrate what can happen when parents put themselves wholeheartedly into changing the way things are going.

Andy (12) had already been driving both his parents and his teachers to distraction for years before we saw him. His parents reported that he was out of their control. Whenever they tried to guide or correct him, he became violent and did things like smashing the car windshield, hitting his parents' Husky dogs, threatening bodily harm to the rest of the family. These incidents often ended with Mr. B.'s hitting the boy and Mrs. B. scolding him for defying her. He had been expelled from two schools because he was as unmanageable at school as at home, and the counselor at the third school advised the parents to put him in a mental hospital for a month's observation.

Andy's setting a poor example for his younger brother Dennis (9) and using Dennis' things without asking was one of the big issues for his parents. One day when Andy calmly picked up his brother's guitar, his father told him he couldn't have it. Andy responded with backtalk and threats which infuriated his father and then, as the argument escalated, he seized his mother's very pregnant pet cat and raced toward the front yard with it, crying out that he would throw it over the fence into the street if his father didn't shut up. Mr. B. caught him just in time to save the cat and, as he did, gave Andy a hearty sideswipe across the back. Andy immediately called the police to complain that he was being beaten. When the police came, he told them he was so angry that he was going to kill his parents that night.

In working with this situation, we gave due thought to the idea of a mental hospital because of Andy's threats and his history of wild behavior. However, we felt we'd much rather help the family live together happily. Two factors influenced us to take this latter direction.

1. Despite all his wild talk, Andy had never actually harmed anyone. The dogs he hit (he slapped them with an open hand) were big and strong and did not look cowed. He had managed to run at precisely the right speed to get himself stopped before actually throwing the cat over the fence. He had not broken the car windshield deliberately but rather by accident in the course of an unrelated scene.

2. We could see things the parents were doing which, if they changed, might make a definite difference in the way things went. Further, the parents were eager to work at making things better. They were miserable in their current situation, and at the same time they certainly did not want to send their boy away. Mr. B. said, "I'll do anything!" We took him at his word, and gave both parents definite instructions to try out.

First, we asked both of them to drop some behaviors, promising that we would coach them on things they could do instead. Mr. B. agreed not to hit Andy again, no matter how intense the provocation (Dad's hitting was giving

Andy a model for violence and he was making full use of it). Mrs. B. agreed to abstain from scolding regardless of what Andy did.

Andy had refused to go to school the day we saw the family, and was playing about the house as we talked. We next told the parents, in Andy's presence, that they were breaking the law by allowing him to stay away from school, that they had no power to make him go, and that since they had already told him to go to school, they should from now on pay *absolutely no attention* to him during school hours. They were to act as though he were not there. (This was designed to deprive Andy of the attention he usually got when he stayed home from school.)

Each parent then made a separate list of the things Andy did that bothered him or her. Each came up with at least eighteen items. With their permission, we list some of them here.

Mr. B.'s list:

Yells at his mother, which infuriates me.

Always contrary. If we all want to go for a pizza, he has to have a hamburger.

Doesn't feel he has to do any work around the house.

Breaks things when he gets mad.

Embarrasses me by throwing fits and tantrums when we go out.

Phones his grandmother long distance and complains about us.

Steals things out of my room. Takes my tools without asking and I never see them again.

Expects me to jump to take him places when and where he wants to go.

Mrs. B.'s list:

Won't get up in time for school. Forgets to bring his homework home so that he won't have to do it.

Leaves a big mess in the kitchen every morning.

Takes off without asking when he knows we're going somewhere.

Doesn't feed the dogs (his job), and is mean to them.

Leaves the bathroom a mess (leaves his dirty clothes lying all over, and doesn't unplug the tub).

Walks in and changes the TV channel while I'm watching it.

Is a total ass when I have company. I feel so ashamed of him.

Acts like an animal when we go out to eat. When we go out with him my stomach is in such a knot I don't enjoy it when we get there.

When I'm on the phone he yells on purpose so I can't hear.

Keeps wanting to go places and won't take no for an answer.

Both parents had these items on their lists, in different words:

Doesn't clean up his side of the boys' bedroom.

Spits everywhere.

Hits the dogs when he's mad.

Won't go to bed on time.

Eggs Dennis into doing dangerous things: stealing, playing with fire or knives, throwing rocks, etc.

For the first week, we worked with Mr. and Mrs. B. on the kid's-life items on their lists. Here's what they did about some of them:

Mr. B.'s complaint that Andy yells at his mother.

Mr. B. agreed to stay out of whatever happened between his wife and Andy. He decided that when Andy's yelling at Mrs. B. bothered him, he would walk out of the room and get busy in his workshop.

Andy's not cleaning his share of the boys' bedroom.

Both parents told both of their sons that they felt the boys could be trusted to work out a way of caring for their room, and that they (the parents) were going to stay out of the problem.

Andy's refusing to get up in time for school, or to bring home his homework.

Mrs. B. told Andy firmly that from now on she was out of the school situation, and would leave it to him and his teachers to work things out between them.

Andy's wanting to go out and not taking "No" for an answer.

Mrs. B. told Andy that she had realized he could take care of himself, and that from now on he was to make the decisions about where he could go.

A few hours after she told him this, Andy tried her out, saying provocatively, "Hey, Mom, I'm going to the bike shop!" Before, she might automatically have said, "No, you can't!" This time she said simply, "Well, that's your decision." Andy seemed startled at getting this answer. A minute later he poked his head in the door and again told her, "Mom, I *said*, I'm going to the bike shop!" Mrs. B. said, "Mm hm." Andy apparently still couldn't believe her, and said angrily, "Mom, didn't you hear what I said? *I'm going to the bike shop!*" Mrs. B. said casually, "Well, I'll see you later then."

Andy never did go to the bike shop, but apparently he really thought about his mother's new stand. For several more weeks he continued to ask her permission to go places in this way, although by the end of that time he had the answer down pat, and he would say, "Hey, Mom, can I go to Joey's house?...I know, I know, that's my decision!"

Staying up late.

The B.'s told both boys that they were old enough to supervise their own bedtime, and from then on said nothing about it at all.

Mr. and Mrs. B. also began focussing much more of their attention on things *they* wanted to do, and much less on Andy. In this first week, they went out for dinner by themselves twice, leaving both boys at home. Andy angrily accused them of never taking him anywhere, and Mr. B. told him he'd be glad to go out with him as soon as he felt sure he wouldn't be embarrassed by Andy's behavior, and not before. The father was fully prepared, the next time Andy made a scene in a restaurant, to walk out and leave him sitting there. Apparently being ready to do so was enough, for he never actually had to do it.

In a week or so, when they were comfortable about having dropped their controls over kid's-life items, Mr. and Mrs. B. began working on parent's-life items.

Mrs. B. picked the morning breakfast messes to work on first. The first time she saw Andy after he'd left these messes was when he came home from school. For several days, then, as soon as she saw him in the afternoon, she said, "Andy, will you please clean up the kitchen?" Andy responded with wisecracks, refusals, accusations ("You don't care about me") and so on, and Mrs. B. followed through with three or four repetitions of her three-part assertive sentence.

Mr. T. chose the problem of Andy's taking his tools. He was all ready to tell Andy that he wanted to feel secure about them, but the problem did not come up again!

The main result of the B.'s work seemed to be this: that Andy liked *being made responsible for himself, and when he was given this responsibility he stopped acting up.*

Within two months after they began working on their problems with Andy, the B.'s reported that there were no longer any real problems. As they put it, Andy had "mellowed out." Both reported feeling closer to him than they ever had. When asked what had happened with the items on their lists, they reported on the ones they could still remember:

School. Andy was going to school regularly. He had got several demerits for forgetting his homework, and there had been one note from a teacher to Mrs. B. She gave this note to Andy, who told her he knew what it was about, that he knew it was his job to take care of it, and that he intended to do so!

Asked about the problem of Andy's not getting up in time for school, Mrs. B. said, "Great."

Yelling at his mother. This had "cut way back." Mr. B. had actually had to leave the room once, when his wife and Andy had an argument. He had a chance to say, "I'm uncomfortable in this situation, and I'm going to leave the room," and do it. Only one other angry incident had occurred in this period: Andy told his folks he had left his bike at school and was going back to get it. Mrs. B. knew the school would be closed and, in a momentary throwback to previous habits, told him he couldn't go. In the old days, said the parents, a real scene would have ensued. This time, instead, Andy simply said huffily, "This is my business!", picked up his coat, and walked out the door to go to the school. His mother thought it over and decided he was right.

Cleaning his room. This was no longer a problem. Dennis was now in charge of cleaning the whole room, as part of a deal the two boys had worked out!

Messes. Andy still sometimes left messes around the house. His father said, "When he does that, I tell him, "I'd like that mess cleaned up." Occasionally he still left the bathroom untidy. Said Mrs. B., "He still needs to be reminded, and as long as I tell him, "*I* didn't leave a mess when I took a bath!" he goes back and cleans it up.

Staying up late. This was no longer a problem. The first few nights in which the parents said nothing about bedtime, both boys stayed up nearly all night. Said Mr. B., "That must have burned them out. Starting with the third night, they went to bed at a very good time and even turned the lights out."

Spitting had disappeared. "We never mentioned that to him, and I have never seen him do it since."

Stealing from the parents' room had stopped. "We just told him our room was off limits."

Demanding to be taken places didn't happen any more. One morning Andy *asked* his father courteously to take him to a soccer game that night, and Mr. B. felt good about doing so.

Wanting to leave the house. Andy was still "independent" about this. If his mother objected to his going out, he would say something like, "I want to, and if I get in trouble, it will be my own fault"—and go.

Not feeding the dogs. Andy still did not feed the dogs; he told his parents he didn't have time to do it before school, and suggested Dennis do it instead. He volunteered to do the yardwork instead!

Molesting the dogs and cat. This hadn't happened in weeks.

Changing TV channels when parents are watching. Andy no longer did this. However, after he stopped doing it, Dennis tried it a few times. His mother told him, "This new system isn't just for Andy. It applies to you, too!"

Embarrassing the parents in front of company. This item had actually reversed itself. Andy's grandfather had visited the family for several weeks, and instead of the harrowing times Andy had always given the family before when this happened, Mrs. B. reported that this time, "He was so good with my father. He cried when his granddad left."

An extra side-effect: The parents had forgotten to list nail-biting as a long time problem. Without a word being said about it, it had disappeared during this period.

In fact, two months after beginning their work, the parents were no longer concerned about Andy's behavior, and were beginning, instead, to use the skills they had learned with Andy to deal with various friends and relatives who, it seemed, had been taking advantage of them. For example, Mrs. B.'s brother regularly borrowed Mr. B.'s car, sometimes without asking, and yet refused to lend Mr. B. his motorcycle, even though that sometimes left the B.'s without transportation. Another relative had come to visit them and had now camped out for many weeks in their garage, where he entertained his girl friends to the accompaniment of liquor, loud music, and much worry for the B.'s about the example he was setting for their sons. It was hard for the B.'s even to say anything to these people, but when they finally did, they were surprised to find that these relationships improved because of it. All of this re-affirmed their new, solid way of dealing with Andy.

It seemed almost too good to be true that Andy should have changed so much because of what the parents had done, and Mr. and Mrs. B. could hardly believe it. They were halfway inclined to attribute the improvement to the fact that Andy had met some new friends and, especially, a very nice girl in his class. We agreed that the new girl friend was a real plus in the situation, but also told the parents we believed the bulk of the credit should go to them and the loving changes they had made.

Kids Are Unique

A great deal of the way a kid develops seems to be determined by something inside the kid. We think the way things went for Mrs. H. and her two children illustrates this.

Mrs. H. is a very easy going, soft hearted, and "mellow" person, and if she had two kids like her son Tom (10) she would probably never have had any problem. Tom was very much like her. However, Tim (12) was very much like her ex-husband—a very self-determined and self-sufficient, rugged, outdoors type of person. Tim loved to play, alone or with a friend, at a nearby creek where he would build shelters of branches, catch mice and lizards, and wade along the creek. Mrs. H. worried not only about all that activity but even that he had to cross a busy street at a light-protected pedestrian cross-walk to get to the creek. He thought her concern was silly and simply did what he wanted to. He also pushed her in all sorts of ways, for example to give him money or buy things he wanted, and she was putty in his hands. He knew that if he made enough of a scene he would get what he wanted, and he was a champion scene-maker.

Mrs. H. was simply not able to take care of herself to the extent needed with Tim. She did make some changes of the sort we coached her to do and found that they were helpful. She also recognized that other things she simply couldn't do would have been beneficial as well. Tim was just too much for her, and she decided to see whether any of her family would be willing to raise him. Her sister and brother-in-law—he is a commercial fisherman in Louisiana—really resonated to Tim, and they were eager to have him. Tim is now being raised by his uncle and aunt, and it is working out very well. Tim fishes with his uncle during the summers and appears to thrive on it. Mrs. H. and Tom are quite comfortable together.

A "Brady Bunch" That Worked

For Mr. and Mrs. M. the principal item on their parent's-life lists was preserving their own relationship together against behaviors of their children and step-children which were driving them apart. Mr. and Mrs. M. had been married about a year when we first met them. They both brought children from previous marriages into the relationship. Mrs. M. had two girls aged 5 and 13, and Mr. M. had a daughter of 12. When they first came for help, the problem, which had started with the two older girls, had become so serious that the parents themselves were close to breaking up. On the face of it, the things that brought the parents to this spot were not serious at all. The two girls would do things like leaving messes in the kitchen or family room, or not putting their bicycles away. The difficulty was that the two parents would treat the two girls differently. Mrs. M. complained that her husband was too harsh a disciplinarian, especially with her daughter, and that he let his own "angel" get away with a lot. Mr. M. said that basic discipline of the girls was his wife's job and she wasn't doing it, so he had to. He resented this, especially as it was her daughter, he said, who caused all the trouble. Mrs. M. was equally emphatic that *his* daughter was the real source of their agony. (We believe they were both right. Kids—and people in general—can be angels or devils selectively depending on the audience).

The girls seemed to play parts well calculated to drive the parents apart. Mr. M.'s daughter did most of the things which particularly annoyed his wife, and his step-daughter knew precisely how to push his button. The incident that brought the situation to a head was triggered by Mrs. M.'s daughter's bike. Mr. M. worked second shift, and when he came home at midnight he liked to open his garage door with his remote control and drive in. One night for the umpteenth time, he found his step-daughter's bike blocking his way. At this point he created a scene which soon involved the whole family.

We persuaded the M.'s to try an approach in which they would focus on taking care of their own relationship: in effect, to stand shoulder to shoulder rather than nose to nose. The two of them were to come up with a uniform method of discipline *if they could*, but if they couldn't, then each was to use his or her own preferred method.* Each kid was to be dealt with by the parent who first noticed any problem, and neither parent was to listen to private tales from a daughter about how evil her step-parent was. The parents also decided to begin referring to each girl as "my daughter" and also to ask that they be called Dad or Mom by their step-daughters rather than by first names.

The M.'s were well motivated to save their marriage because it was basically a good one. Consequently they were able to begin changing the way they were with their daughters. For example, Mrs. M. would announce to both girls, "I want the playroom kept clean of dirty dishes," and after the usual early responses parents get with that approach ("I didn't do it!" "I didn't either!") she succeeded to a large extent in having the place cleaner. An important side effect was that she learned that she didn't really care

---

* In all of our work, we emphasize that it is not necessary for parents to adopt a uniform attitude in dealing with the kids, as long as there is not deliberate sabotage. For example, the bicycles were Mr. M.'s problem. If having them left in the middle of the garage floor didn't bother Mrs. M. she could simply do nothing about them and let it be a problem the girls would have with Mr. M. Of course, she should refrain from encouraging the girls to be careless about the bikes, directly or indirectly—that's sabotage—but simply not get involved one way or the other.

as much as she thought she did that it had to be perfectly neat.

The father announced to both girls that if he saw any bicycle blocking his car, he would pay no attention to whose it was, but would wake both girls to come and put it away. And he did. As you might imagine, the bicycles very soon stopped blocking his path at night.

Mr. and Mrs. M. have now been married for an additional five years, and the two older girls are pretty well grown up. Very early, the girls gave up their provocative behaviors and each parent began experiencing loving feelings towards both girls. The favoritism disappeared. The parents are quite happy together, and they're both happy with all three girls. The girls have long since given up the behaviors that were dividing the parents and seem to be quite comfortable in the family.

A "Brady Bunch" That Didn't Work

Not all "Brady Bunch" families are as successful as the M.'s. The L. family did not work out.

Mr. and Mrs. L. each brought a 14 year old son into their marriage. One of them, Mr. L.'s son, was particularly active in what seemed like an attempt to cause problems between the parents. He was extremely surly with his step-mother, and in private talks with us he made it very clear that he wanted his original mother and his father to get together again, even though he knew it was very unlikely. He also said that even if his step-mother treated him as well as she treated his stepbrother (which he felt was excellent treatment), he would still not be nice to her.

Despite the fact that each of the parents recognized that the behavior of the boys, particularly the father's boy, was driving a wedge between them, they have not been able to change the way they deal with them—to turn responsibilities for their own actions over to the boys and to stand together as a team to deal with the very important parent's-life item of damage to their relationship. In this instance, the only really major problem was the surliness of one of the boys in the presence of his step-mother. However, the parents were not able to revise the way they do things, and they are, as of this writing, on the verge of separating.

A Long-Term Effort

Mrs. Z. was strongly into the habit of ignoring her own wants and focussing most of her energy on controlling her son's life, instead. Her story demonstrates how even a deeply ingrained habit like this can be changed over time and an improved way of living result.

Mrs. Z., a computer programmer, had raised her 14 year old son Ted by herself, almost from his infancy. His father was long gone and nobody knew anything of his whereabouts. Mrs. Z. also had a crippled leg which meant that, except for short distances, she had to walk using crutches. She spent much of her energy worrying about whether Ted was doing "right," and her imagination was most vivid. She originally called for counselling help for Ted because she was suspicious that he was going to get an 11 year old girl, who lived in a neighboring apartment, pregnant. She had no real evidence for her belief that there was sexual activity going on and when we looked into the matter, it seemed highly unlikely. Yet she worried, worried, worried, about what would happen if this pregnancy occurred—would she be responsible; what would happen to Ted; what would the other mother do to her, and so forth. She could imagine everyone in town reading about the situation in the newspaper, Ted's being named as the father, his having to marry the little girl and never finishing school, having to live all his life as a laborer, and so on. Other problems that bothered her had to do with the way the two of them lived together and Ted's not doing his fair share of the work. Because of her leg she could not carry out the garbage and she had difficulty cleaning the bathtub. Those and some cleaning up chores were established as Ted's jobs, but he always shirked them.

Ted struck us as a basically solid boy, with a minor tendency to get into some mischief but generally doing well in school and getting an occasional lawn-mowing job on his own initiative. His main problem was that his mother was so tightly controlling that he had very little feeling of running his own life. Even when he would get his lawn-mowing jobs, his mother would ride herd on him to make sure he did them exactly as she thought was right, that his customers were completely satisfied, and so forth. She worried that they wouldn't be.

Mrs. Z. had had to make many personal sacrifices in order to raise Ted to adolescence, and in the process she had become almost entirely focussed on his life and welfare and had nearly forgotten what her own wants might be. In our work with her, we coached her on the very difficult task of dropping controls over Ted's life and picking up instead the responsibility for making her own life happy.

Mrs. Z. and we worked together for a long time. Over a period of approximately two years she very gradually changed, and little by little was able to let Ted run more of his own life. Each new item that came up was a struggle for her. He wanted to get a job. He wanted to go camping with an older boy whom she acknowledged was a competent and experienced camper and whom she liked. He wanted to take a girl to a movie. He wanted to enter a science fair. Each instance caused her to worry, and she was brilliant at imagining all sorts of exotic catastrophes that might ensue. However, she coped with each item as it arose and by the end of the two year period could look back with a bit of amusement at her earlier self. She was able to smile at the memory of her worry about Ted's getting the little girl pregnant, and to feel satisfied that yes, indeed; he was growing up to be a pretty nice boy—even though he was doing things on his own and she had essentially given up on control of his-life items.

During this period, she also began taking much better care of her own life. She learned that she loved going on weekend excursions with two women friends, and began doing so. She enjoyed going to plays and concerts, and bought pairs of season tickets. If Ted wanted to go, which he often did, she invited him. If not, she found someone else to go with her. She engineered a modest shift in her work situation which gave her much greater satisfaction in her job. She realized she hated their apartment, and moved to a nicer one, telling Ted she would be looking for some extra help in paying for it. Ted, too, wanted to live in a better apartment, and enthusiastically agreed to this.

Ted is now approaching 17, a senior in high school, and had held down a job for the past year in a fast food service where he is now a manager. Sometimes he doesn't take the garbage out spontaneously, but one reminder is usually all it takes. The tub-cleaning problem has disappeared because their new apartment has a shower, which they both prefer anyway, and he washes the shower out to her satisfaction, using his washrag and his foot. They are quite happy together, and they both enjoy going to dinner and a concert together. He has developed a set of friends where they now live and she is quite content with them. Mrs. Z. took approximately two years to truly decide that yes, it was good for the two of them that she run her life and that she let him run his, and she is now reaping the harvest of that decision.

Index

Abusing favors: 103, 119–124

Appearance, kid's: 16, 28

Assertive statement, three-part: 140

Attitude, kid's: 17, 19, 31, 103, 116–119

Attitude, parent's: xv, 4, 6–11, 45–49, 67, 88–89

Baths, won't take: 16, 20

Breaking things: 28, 85, 127, 134, 137

Car, use of: 85, 119–124

Chores: 2, 17, 85, 127, 129 f.

Closeness, between kid and parent: 183

Consistency, between parents: 180

Cooperation between parents: 116

Damages, parental liability for: 26

Dangers, for kid: 49–50, 61, 64–65

Daring thoughts: 55, 73

Decision-making ability: 41–44, 55–56

Dress, unkempt: 16, 28

Encounter, fear of: 96–99

Equal relationships: 89–93, 95

Establishing credibility: 128–129, 153–159

Establishing fairness: 128, 129–135

Family, doing things with: 2, 17, 24, 177

Favors, refusing: 121–124

Fights, with siblings: 17, 21–22

Freeloading: 30, 86, 95, 127, 134

Friends, older: 17

Friends, "undesirable": 2, 17, 24–25

Goals, parent's: 12–14

Gordon, Dr. Thomas: xiv

Guidance, by parent: 180

"Have to" in speech: 77

Heartening, self: 6–11

Homework, kid's: 17, 30

House, bringing kids in: 17, 86, 127, 130 f., 160

Houses, breaking into: 18, 29

I-statements: 37, 61–63, 73–76, 103 f.

204

Joyriding: 18, 29
Kid's-life list: 18 f., 37
Legal aspects: 29, 95–6, 170
Limits, setting: 181
Liquor: 17, 27, 61–63, 127
Love, communicating: 42–45
Love, levels of: 41–43
Lying: 2, 31, 103–106
Marijuana: 2, 17, 27, 85, 127, 137
Messes, making: 2, 16, 85, 127, 192, 193–4
Money, demanding: 17, 85
Name-calling: 17, 31, 103, 113–116
Negative attention: 57–58, 104 f.
Negatives, in speech: 77–78
Neglecting own things: 17, 20–21
Noisy: 22, 23, 95, 127, 130 f.
Parent Effectiveness Training: xiv
Parent, happiness of: 84, 87
Parent, openness of: 99–101
Parent, privacy of: 19, 31, 71, 95
Parents, cooperation between: 16, 184, 197–200
Parents, obligations of: 37
Parent's feelings of guilt: inadequacy, shame: xii–xiii, 4, 11–12, 172–3
Parent-s-life list: 85 f., 127 f.
Parent's relationship with partner: 18, 86, 95, 191

Parent's rights: 12, 71, 93–95, 184
Parent's things, borrowing, stealing, giving away: 16, 85
Pets, won't feed or clean up: 16, 85, 122, 127, 130 f., 159
Phone, problems with: 17, 85, 127, 137, 160, 187
Police, involvement with: 11, 27, 61–63
Pregnancy: 2, 17, 27, 127
Problems, list of: 16–18
Questions parents ask: 35, 180 f.
Reinforcing misbehavior: 102 f.
Relaxation: 7–11
Rights, of parents: 12, 71, 93–95, 184
Room, cleaning: 17, 23, 191, 193
Running away: 2, 17, 25–26
School, failing: 17, 30, 63
Self-image, kid's: 182
Selfishness, of caring for oneself: 182
Sexual activity: 2, 17, 27
Shoplifting: 2, 18, 29
"Should" in speech: 77
Smoking: 17, 18, 27, 127
Sneaking out at night: 17, 28
Spontaneity: 78–79
Spouse won't cooperate: 6, 184
Staying up late: 16, 19, 192, 194

Stealing, from parents: 2, 16-17, 85, 103, 107-112, 127, 160, 194

Stealing, from siblings: 112

Step-parenting: 197-199

Strike, parental: 129, 166-172

Suicide threats: 18, 113-116

Swearing: 2, 17, 85, 103, 113-116, 130 f.

Tantrums: 17, 22-23

Threats: 17, 113-116

Triggering misbehavior: 102 f.

Television: 17, 19-20, 30

Truancy: 2, 30, 61-63, 190-191, 193

Unpredictability of kid: 45

Unpredictability of parent: 148-152

Verbal behavior of kids: 31, 103, 113-116

Violence by kid: 17, 95; toward kid: 189

Visualizing: 8-11

Wants to be by oneself (kid): 2, 17, 24

About the authors

Jean and Bob Bayard have been a team for thirty-six years. Both psychologists, they have a clinical practice together in California. They have raised five children together; when their youngest reached eighteen, they had had thirty-two consecutive years of kid raising. By that time they had experienced at first hand most of the problems they discuss in this book.

Jean is a psychotherapist and specializes in helping women fulfill their full potential. She is a writer, a serious student of philosophy, and she supports Greenpeace and every sincere attempt to take care of human beings and their world.

Bob's first career was as a physicist and manager of technical research and development. It included a year spent as a United Nations Technical Assistance Expert in Thailand. In 1975, at the age of fifty-five, he took his second Ph.D., in psychology, and has been working as a psychotherapist ever since. He specializes in problems of families and of couples.

APR 1983
RECEIVED
JOHN STEINBECK
LIBRARY

SALINAS PUBLIC LIBRARY

3 3550 00100 8742